Memoirs of Vice Admiral
James A. Sagerholm, USN (Ret.)

From
GREEN HILLS
to BLUE SEAS

12/20/2015

To John and Kathleen,
With warmest regards,
Jim Sagerholm

JAMES A. SAGERHOLM

outskirtspress
DENVER, COLORADO

From Green Hills to Blue Seas
Memoirs of Vice Admiral James A. Sagerholm, USN (Ret.)

Outskirts Press, Inc.
http://www.outskirtspress.com

ISBN: 978-1-4787-5295-0

Outskirts Press and the "OP" logo are trademarks belonging to Outskirts Press, Inc.

Foreword

I have written these memoirs at the request of my grandson, Captain Dane Sagerholm, USMC., and they are my personal recollections of the events described herein. Any errors of fact are strictly mine.

Knowing what one's forebears did in life gives a family a sense of continuity as well as hints as to why their own traits are as they are. History, whether of family or of a culture, helps in understanding the why of things, and is an important facet of education that must be given adequate study. It is my hope that my twelve grandchildren may find in these pages some guidance that will help them in the future, and that they will see the value of the family as the foundation of society. May God bless them, and may they always let God be at their side.

J. A. Sagerholm

Table of Contents

PART I.
FROM GREEN HILLS

1

Uniontown, Pennsylvania

The winter of 1927-1928 was reportedly one of the worst on record, with heavy snowstorms and below-freezing temperatures, at least that's what I was told.

It was still dark when Dr. John Robinson, the family physician, arrived at the home of Mr. and Mrs. F. Norris Sagerholm, Sr., at 76 South Gallatin Avenue, in the small town of Uniontown, located some 40 miles south of Pittsburgh, in the soft coal mining fields of southwestern Pennsylvania. The snow had finally stopped after several days of continuous blizzard conditions, and Dr. Robinson drove to the house with some difficulty on the snow-packed streets. The hour was about five a.m., and Mrs. Sagerholm had been in labor with her second child for over four hours.

Dr. Robinson was a general practitioner in the full sense of the term; he was a surgeon, an obstetrician, a counselor for disturbed patients, and a strong support for the families he served. He never hesitated to come to the house of a patient, and was a highly respected and valued member of the community.

At approximately seven-thirty a.m., Dr. Robinson delivered a baby boy to the Sagerholm family; the date was Friday, December 23, 1927. Several weeks later, the baby was christened James Alvin Sagerholm by Father Bernard Kenna, pastor of St. John's Roman Catholic Church.

Frankly, although I am sure I was there, I do not remember a thing about December 23, 1927, nor about the baptism, but since my parents told me what I have written, I assume it is true.

When I was two or so, we moved to the outskirts of Uniontown in a section named Homewood Terrace. There I became buddies with the teen-age son of one of our neighbors, the Sheaffer family. Homer and I used to raid his father's strawberry patch, and I invariably was detected later as being guilty of such by the red ring around my mouth. Those juicy strawberries were too tempting to avoid, and Homer and I continued our forays despite the scoldings received. Homer "Shaper" and I were incorrigible in that regard.

Three years later, we moved back to the convenience of living near the downtown section where the shops were located, there being no malls in those days. Our new address was 70 South Gallatin Avenue, just a few doors from where I was born. The Great Depression was in its third year, and prices of things had deflated considerably. The house we moved into had been converted into a duplex by closing off the top of the stairway and adding a kitchen to the upstairs unit as well as an outside set of stairs, while adding a bathroom to the downstairs unit. We lived in the downstairs, which had the advantage of a full basement, but it also entailed my father keeping the furnace stoked with coal in the winter since it was the only source of heat for both units. We had two bedrooms, a living room, and a full kitchen, with all rooms having hardwood floors and high ceilings. A large front porch sat some six feet above the ground, requiring nine steps to reach the porch. There was a small porch in the back, with an outside pantry off the back porch in which was kept our icebox. The kitchen had large built-in cupboards, a gas stove, a large sink and linoleum flooring. The rent was $25.00 per month.

When spring arrived with warmer weather, and continuing through the summer and fall, it was necessary to have a 50 lb. block of ice delivered every three days for the ice box. On hot days, we would snare chips of ice from the ice truck while the delivery man was placing the block of ice in the ice box. Milk was delivered daily by a horse-drawn wagon. The milk was in quart glass bottles, with the heavy cream in the top of the bottle. The cream was drawn off and used for coffee or tea, and on rare occasions, for cereal. We fed apples to the horse, a white draft horse, very gentle, and he would wait for us to feed him before he pulled away to the next stop. The milkman was kind and patient with us, and never interfered with our feeding his horse. The horse knew every stop, and the only time he needed direction from the milkman was when there was a change of customers. We called the horse "Whitey," but we never bothered to ask what his real name was. A quart of milk cost around a dime. The ice was a dollar a week.

Across the street was Fingerett's Bakery, owned and operated by Sam Fingerett, a burly Jewish man who, with his wife and two daughters, lived in the apartment above the bakery. There were rumors that Mr. Fingerett was a "Bolshevik," a Communist. He may or may not have been, but whatever the case, there was a weekly gathering of six or so men at the apartment. The gathering could have been for a weekly poker game, but it offered some substance to the rumors, especially since the men looked suspicious to us kids.

Sam, for some reason, decided to sell the bakery, and in 1938, as I recall, it became Young's Bakery. The new owner was Carl Jung, who changed his name to Young. He was a big, kindly German from Berlin, who decided to emigrate to the United States when he saw what Hitler was doing in Germany. He and his wife bought the house where I was born, and they sort of adopted me. Mr. Young fed me fresh-baked cookies, and every now and then, he would take me to the Penn Theater on Main Street to see the Saturday afternoon double feature, which always was a combination of a movie featuring Hopalong Cassidy and another Western with Tom Mix or John Wayne. The good guys always wore white ten gallon hats (the bad guys wore black), and had horses that were faithful to their masters and saved them time and time again from seemingly impossible situations. Mr. Young loved those Westerns. Their only child was a grown daughter who was married to an officer in the German army. Mrs. Young went to daily Mass to pray for her daughter and her grandchildren. I never knew what happened to them as a result of the war.

Mr. Young suffered a stroke in 1941, and died in the house where I was born. The bakery is still there, and is still called Young's Bakery although it has changed hands several times. The house in which we lived has long since been torn down to make way for the Hagan Ice Cream plant, which now occupies the entire block where our home was located. The ice cream plant was much smaller when we lived there, and was in the rear of the block, facing an alley that ran parallel to our street. The delicious smell of chocolate would waft through the entire block some times. In the summer, we could go to the plant and get popsicles for a nickel.

My brother and I attended St. John's School, where we were taught by the Sisters of St. Joseph, whose motherhouse was at Gallitzen, Pa., north of Pittsburgh. I started in the first grade in September 1933, at the age of five, so I was the youngest in the class. The parish had been built from the ground up by the Irish who had come to Uniontown in the 1890's, with Father Kenna, their pastor in Ireland. He was a strict priest, and knew everyone in the parish, so when the depression came, he made a practice of personally taking the collection at every Mass on Sunday, stopping only at those who had, and passing those who had not. He would come out for the collection garbed in his cassock and lace surplice, wearing his biretta, and flanked by the two altar boys carrying lighted candles. One Sunday, my brother and I were serving at 9 o'clock Mass, and we were alongside Father Kenna while he took up the collection. He came to Mr. Cray, who was a banker and probably the wealthiest man in the parish. Old Jim Cray sat there looking straight ahead and not making any move to place an offering in the basket. Father Kenna tapped him on the chest with the basket, but there was no response from Mr. Cray. Father Kenna tapped him again a bit harder, and Cray's face turned red, but he made no gesture of offering. Father rapped him again on the chest. Obviously angry, Cray jammed his hand into his vest pocket and pulled out a coin that he threw into the basket. Then he was horrified to see that he had thrown his lucky twenty-dollar gold piece instead of the half-dollar he had intended. He started to reach into the basket to retrieve it but Father Kenna blocked his hand, saying, "Uh-uh, it belongs to God now." I heard later that Father Kenna allowed Mr. Cray to buy it back at the cost of a twenty-dollar bill.

When I was in the seventh grade, a new girl named Peggy O'Connor arrived in our class, having come from Pittsburgh with her family. Her father was with Woolworth's and was the new district manager. I thought she was pretty cute, so one day I wrote a little poem and passed it across the schoolroom to her. It read, "Roses are red, your eyes are blue, I would like to get to know you." Back came the note with the short comment, "My eyes are brown." I could have said I was blinded by her looks or some equally clever rejoinder, but I didn't think of that until later, so that was the end of my romantic overture to Miss O'Connor.

Not being Irish, I was definitely one of the minority members of the class; as a result, I was in a fist fight every now and then. One afternoon after school, a lad named George Fallon and I were flailing away at each other out behind the school, not really doing much damage, when I heard the town hall clock striking four. My mother was pretty strict about our being home from school not later than 4:15, so I stepped back, dropped my arms, and told George that we would have to finish our bout the next day. George well understood the consequences if I were late, and immediately agreed to stop, much to the disappointment of the crowd. We never did resume the fight, and became good friends. I don't remember what the fight was about.

In September 1941, I entered St. John's High School in the ninth grade. The high school principal was Sister DeChantal, very strict and no nonsense. My homeroom teacher was Sister Marie Collette, young and very nice. One afternoon, I arrived back at school from lunch about fifteen minutes before classes resumed. My desk was in the front, and when I sat down, I saw that someone had left a tinfoil gum wrapper on my desk. As I sat there, waiting for the class to return, I idly tore off strips of the tinfoil and rolled the strips into tiny balls. I have no idea why I did this other than being somewhat bored.

As the class began arriving, Sister Marie Collette also came in. Almost immediately, she noticed the small pile of tinfoil balls on my desk, and she exclaimed, "James, are you throwing spitballs?" I was shocked, and denied doing any such thing. She pointed at the pile on my desk and demanded to know why I had them. I was at a loss to explain, so she took that as evidence of my intent to throw spitballs, and marched me down the hall to the principal's office. After hearing the charges against me, Sister DeChantal ordered me to apologize to Sister Marie Collette, and told me to promise never to throw spitballs again. I said I had never thrown any spitballs and so I had nothing to apologize for or to promise. Sister DeChantal stood up and took me out into the hall where there was a bench outside her office. She told me I could not return to the home room until I apologized, and in the meantime, I was to sit on that bench. So down I sat, and a tearful Sister Marie Collette went back to the class.

That was on a Tuesday, and come Friday, I was still sitting on the bench, a source of much amusement to the students, who passed me every hour when classes changed. My classmates kept me informed of homework and the day's lessons, so all I missed were the actual classroom lectures from the teachers. My brother was a senior, and he thought the whole situation was very funny, but he never said anything about it at home, knowing that the parental wrath would be much worse than what I was enduring at school.

Just after lunch that Friday, both Sister DeChantal and Sister Marie Collette arrived together. Sister DeChantal gave me a disgusted look and went into her office. Sister Marie Collette came over to me and said she was upset that I was still not with the class. I said I was sorry to hear that she was upset, and before I could say anything more, she exclaimed, "James! You apologized!" I was about to deny that when she burst into the principal's office and shouted, "Sister! James has apologized!" Then she grabbed my arm and hustled me down the hall to the homeroom, and when the class saw me coming in with a beaming Sister Marie Collette, they clapped and cheered. I knew I had not apologized for the spitballs, but fate was playing the hand, so I acknowledged the cheers and dropped into my desk seat. That's how my spitball adventure finally ended.

On Sunday afternoon, 7 December, 1941, my parents, my brother and I were out driving the back roads of the area, admiring the freshly fallen snow. The car radio was on, and shortly after 4 p.m., the program was interrupted by the announcement that the Japanese had attacked Pearl Harbor. My father immediately headed for home, where we gathered in front of the radio and listened to the stream of news now coming in. It was clear that the United States was now in the war that had erupted in Europe when Hitler, the leader of Germany, invaded Poland on 1 September, 1939. On December 8th, President Roosevelt requested Congress to declare war against Japan, calling the day of the attack a "day that will live in infamy." The president vowed that we would see it through to the final victory, "so help us, God!"

It was an electrifying event, and young men lined up in front of the recruiting stations to volunteer. The draft had already been enacted and now it went into high gear; within a few months it seemed as if all the young men were gone, only to reappear in uniforms of khaki, or Navy blue or Marine green, as they took leave before going into the war. There was a total unity of purpose among the people, a unity that dispelled all isolationist tendencies overnight. There was never a doubt that we would ultimately prevail.

My brother was sixteen and a senior in high school. My parents obviously were worried about him, but they accepted the reality of knowing that most families would have a member in the war.

2 | Baltimore

In March, 1942, my father went to Baltimore to work at the Glenn L. Martin Aircraft Company. They were building seaplanes for the Navy and bombers for the Army Air Corps, and were expanding production rapidly. Dad was an accountant, and was assigned to the office that measured production versus time, called the Time Study Department. Their purpose was to find bottlenecks and remove them. We stayed in Uniontown until school finished in June, when my brother graduated. To pay for the move to Baltimore, Mother sold our 8-cylinder deluxe Chrysler sedan for $800 to the Rossi family. That car was my dad's pride and joy, but the times required sacrifices, and he willingly gave his consent to sell the car.

On a bright sunny day in June 1942, we went to the bus station in Uniontown and boarded the bus for the trip to Baltimore. Our Blocher cousins were there to see us off, and soon we were rolling along U.S. Route 40, going over the Alleghenies to a new life.

After six hours or so, we arrived in Baltimore, driving through the busy downtown to the bus station where my dad was waiting for us. The station was built in the Art Deco style, and still stands as part of the Maryland Historical Society property. We each had a suitcase and boarding the streetcar was a chore, but we made it and rode through town to the northwest section of Baltimore, an area called Forest Park. Dad had rented an apartment in the Garrisonian Apartments on Garrison Boulevard, just south of the intersection with Liberty Heights

Avenue. That was in June of 1942, and my parents lived there until my father's untimely death on 6 November 1960.

There was a block-long business section on Liberty Heights Avenue, beginning at the intersection with Garrison Boulevard and running east to Ayrdale Avenue. One of the businesses was Shure's Drugstore. Shure's had a sign in the window announcing that they were hiring soda fountain attendants, or "soda jerks" as they were called then.

Before we moved from Uniontown, I had worked the previous summer at Zimmerman's Nut and Ice Cream Shop. I was only thirteen, but nobody worried about that sort of thing then, probably because of the recent Depression when everyone in a family had to work to make ends meet. My first day on the job, the owner, "Pap" Zimmerman, told me that as an employee, I could have all the nuts and ice cream I wanted. As wise old Mr. Zimmerman expected, I stuffed myself to the point that I didn't want another bite of ice cream or another nut.

I had learned how to make sundaes, banana splits and milkshakes, as well as sandwiches, so I entered Shure's with the confidence of a veteran soda attendant, and I walked up to the pharmacist, who happened to be "Doc" Irving Shure, youngest son of the owner. At age fourteen, I was already six feet tall, but weighed only about 140 pounds. I told Doc Shure that I was applying for the job at the soda fountain, and added that I had a year's experience. He looked me over, picked up a 50-pound bag of sugar, dropped it on my shoulder, and told me to follow him. He headed down a stairway in the rear of the store and I staggered after him, precariously keeping my balance going down the stairs. We entered the basement where there was a gas range with a large kettle beside it. A large sink was opposite the stove. He told me to drop the bag of sugar which I did with great alacrity, feeling as if I were going to float in the air once the weight of the bag was gone. He asked me if I knew how to make simple syrup, the base for all the flavored syrups, and I allowed as how I certainly did. I filled the kettle with five gallons of water, and emptied the bag of sugar into the water. Turning on the gas burner, I stirred the mixture with a wooden paddle until the sugar had completely dissolved, and there were now five gallons of simple syrup. So I was hired, having passed Doc Shure's practical exam.

I had to wear a white shirt with the sleeves rolled to just above the elbows, a black bow tie, and a white apron. I also had a name tag with "Jimmy" printed on it. Mr. Shure insisted that the name tag was to help the customers get to know us, but we knew that it actually was to let a customer identify an employee who had not provided good service. He wasn't fooling us, not a bit.

I worked from 12 noon until the close of business at 10 p.m., at the hourly wage of thirty two cents an hour, less the deduction for Social Security, six days a week, alternating Saturdays and Sundays, so my take-home pay per week was about seventeen dollars. I worked a total of twelve weeks that summer, stopping just before school started, which was the day after Labor Day. By the end of summer, I had saved well over one hundred dollars, enough to buy clothes for school and still have some left over for recreation or whatever. I worked there that summer and the following summer.

One afternoon, I was chatting with a lad my age who came in for a coke about every afternoon, name of Dickie Dutton. In walked a blonde, a brunette, and a redhead, and they all knew Dutton. They ordered cokes, were there about twenty minutes, and then left. Dutton was still there, so I asked him for their names and phone numbers. I was especially attracted to the brunette whose name was Peggy Herrlich. The blonde was Ruth Ritterhoff and the redhead was Nancy Fitzsimmons. Throughout the rest of the summer they would come in and have a coke or milkshake, and we chatted a bit, but that was all the socializing I did with the fair sex that summer. However, that chance encounter was to have far-reaching implications for the rest of my life.

I bought a used bike for ten dollars and rode all over the city and out into the county. There was not a lot of traffic on the roads, gas being rationed, so biking was an easy thing to do then. The main means of transportation was the city trolley and bus system. For ten cents, one could travel from one end of the system to another, transferring between trolley and bus as necessary. Snow never stopped the trolley cars so there was never an excuse for missing school due to snow.

I enrolled in the Advanced College Prep Course at Baltimore Polytechnic Institute, located then on North Avenue at Calvert Street. It was a public high school, all boys, with a student body of some 2300 boys who came from all sections of Baltimore. The "A" course was four years, while the College Prep Course, the "B" course, and the General Technical Course, the "G" course, were each three years. Graduates of the "A" course could enter college in the engineering majors at the sophomore level, having completed credits in thermodynamics, strength of materials, integral and differential calculus, and electricity, as well as four years of English, two years of a foreign language, and four years of history. All this was in addition to algebra, plane and solid geometry, plane and solid trigonometry, analytic geometry, physics and chemistry. We also had three years of shop in wood, sheet metal, foundry and machine shop. Mechanical drawing for the first three years was followed by a year of surveying and plat drawing from our survey. Poly was one of the top three boys' technical high schools in the country. Our big rival was Baltimore City College, which was the liberal arts counterpart of Poly's engineering curriculum. Both schools were magnet schools before there ever was such a term. Their football rivalry started in 1888, and has continued unbroken ever since, one of the oldest high school rivalries in the nation. Both schools are now co-ed, and both are still among the best in the state. My four years at Poly were to have a profound impact, preparing me better than I realized at the time for my studies at the Naval Academy, and providing me disciplined study and work habits that have benefited me for the rest of my life.

I lettered in track, running the quarter mile, the mile relay, and the half mile. Near the end of my sophomore year, when the track season ended, the captain of the team, Howie Taylor, announced that he was having a party at his home in the Pimlico area of Baltimore, and we were each expected to bring a date. This was the spring of 1944, two years after I had obtained the names and phone numbers from Dickie Dutton but I had never called anyone. My first two years at Poly were study, study, study, with work during the summers, so I did not know any girls other than my brief acquaintance with the Shure's Drugstore trio. Somehow, I had saved the information from Dutton, so I phoned the brunette, Peggy Herrlich, and said that this was Jimmy Sagerholm calling. She asked, "Do I know you?" I told her of our having met at Shure's when I worked there, and she exclaimed, "Oh, you're Jimmy Shure!" Seems the girls had given me that name because they didn't know my last name. After getting the name straightened out, I asked her to go to the track team party with me, and to my relief, she assented to do so. She was a terrific first date, very pretty, relaxed and chatty, making it easy for me to be with her. She was also a marvelous dancer. She became my steady date.

The summer of 1944, I worked with a Poly classmate and good friend, Bill Ruff, whose father was a building contractor. Mr. Ruff put us to work on a job at Aberdeen Proving Ground, an Army installation north of Baltimore. The job consisted of building a wooden trestle about a hundred yards long, backed by a thick berm of dirt. The trestle carried a moving car on rails, with a square target on the car, the purpose of which was to test various guns for use in tanks. Concrete shelters at each end of the trestle housed the mechanism for pulling the target car back and forth. Another concrete shelter sat across from the trestle on the opposite side of the range, used by the observers of the tests. The first item to be constructed was the berm, done by a bulldozer operated by a Mexican named Diego. Bill and I manned a theodolite for surveying the berm to ensure that it complied with the blueprint. With the berm completed, we began construction of the three concrete shelters. This entailed first putting together the steel reinforcing bars around which would be poured the concrete. The bars had to be held together with snips of wire wound around the bars where they criss-crossed, forming a mat of steel bars. Heavy wooden forms were then placed on the site where the concrete wall was to be, the mat was lowered between the forms, and the concrete was then poured down between the forms and around the steel bars. The final stage of the project was building the trestle, made of the same type of wood used in railroad trestles, with wooden ties laid on the surface upon which were laid the iron rails. The entire trestle had to be coated with creosote as a preservative. We started in early June and completed the work in late August. Working with us were German POWs from the Afrika Korps, most of them just a few years older than us. The most difficult job was applying the creosote in the boiling hot sun of August, with the creosote inevitably dripping onto our dungarees. My mother made me remove the dungarees as soon as I entered our apartment, and immediately washed them. I went through two pairs of dungarees in three weeks.

The summer of 1945, I decided to find work that would not be so physically demanding, so I applied at the neighborhood theater, the Ambassador, for the usher position they had advertised, and I was hired. As it turned out, ushering was a nine hour stint, starting at one p.m., a half hour before the theater opened, and ending at ten p.m. , working four days a week We were allowed two ten minute breaks and one twenty minute supper break during that time. We were provided a white mess jacket and black trousers, and had to wear a white shirt with a black bow tie, and black shoes. I was on when the news came in that Japan had surrendered. The manager stopped the movie, turned on the lights, and announced the good news. The audience started cheering and marching around the theater, and were soon joined by a line of others from the outside. The demonstration lasted well over an hour, and when we finally got the theater back in operation, there was only time for one showing of the main feature, but nobody was in the audience. So the manager decided to call it a day, and off we went to join the celebrations that were still going on. The war with all its many sacrifices was now ended, and everyone seemed to have difficulty in fully grasping what that meant. It took several days for us to finally realize that we were entering a new era of history, one with challenges of a different sort, but challenges that were just as threatening to our country.

The Poly track team competed against the Naval Academy Plebe team each year, and my trip to the Academy my sophomore year was the beginning of my love affair with the Navy. From that day on, I knew that I wanted nothing more than to be a midshipman and then to serve in the Navy as an officer. I am not really sure what specifically attracted me, most likely it was the combination of the strong sense of tradition that the Academy embodied, together with the war and the whole setting of the Brigade of Midshipmen against the majestic background of Bancroft Hall and the monument-studded Yard. The huge bowls of creamy rich home-made vanilla ice cream we received after the meets also had an effect. Whatever it was, I was hooked. So it was that during my senior year at Poly I tried to obtain a nomination from one or the other of the Maryland senators and the Congressman for our district, but without success. All told me that their quotas for 1946 were already filled, and to come back next year.

On the advice of the school counselor, I had taken the national competitive examination for the Coast Guard Academy which did not require a Congressional nomination. Norman Venske, a Poly class-mate, also took the Coast Guard exam. In early June, Norm and I were notified that we had finished among the top ten in the nation, and we were directed to take a physical at the US Public Health Hospital in Baltimore. I learned that the vision in my right eye was 20/30, which disqualified me for not only the Coast Guard Academy but the Naval Academy as well. Norm passed the physical, went to New London and on to a very successful career in the Coast Guard, becoming a leading authority on polar operations. He retired in the rank of rear admiral.

Since my real desire was Annapolis, I was not dismayed about being denied New London, but I was concerned about being dis-qualified for the Naval Academy. Nevertheless, I was convinced that somehow I was going to be a midshipman.

My brother had enlisted in the Navy shortly before his eighteenth birthday in April 1943. After a series of schools in the Navy, he be-came a flight engineer on the Martin Mariner seaplane with the rate of Aviation Machinist's Mate 2/c. His squadron participated in the Marianas campaign in 1944, during which he earned the Air Medal. Shortly after the end of the campaign, his commanding officer asked him if he would be interested in attending the Naval Academy. He explained that the secretary of the Navy annually appointed about one hundred enlisted men to the Academy from the Navy and Marine Corps, after the appointees had successfully completed the nine month course at the Naval Academy Preparatory School (NAPS). Each summer, the Bureau of Naval Personnel solicited Academy applicants from those who had completed at least one year of enlisted service. On the urging of his plane commander, Sag agreed to apply, and a month later, he received orders to NAPS, then located at Bainbridge, Maryland. In June of 1945, he was sworn in as a midshipman in the class of 1949. Thus I knew that there was another route for gaining an appointment. I was convinced that I could follow the same route as my brother, regardless of my right eye, so I enlisted in the Navy for four years, and on 15 July 1946, I arrived at Bainbridge for boot training. I would wear Navy blue for the next 39 years.

3 | Navy Enlisted Service

I will never forget that first night at Bainbridge. We had arrived late in the afternoon, and by the time we were checked in, it was time for the evening meal, and then to our temporary barracks for the night. We were still in civilian clothes, and all we were issued was a set of sheets, a mattress cover, a pillowcase and a blanket. The bunks were wooden frame, two bunks high; I slept in an upper bunk. I remember looking up at the overhead (ceiling to landlubbers) and wondering just what I had done and was it the right thing. If I didn't make the Academy, I would be serving four years as an enlisted man, which was alright, but then what?

The next morning we were rousted out of our bunks by a seaman who told us to follow him. We went to breakfast in a mess hall being used by boots, and were constantly greeted by the refrain, "You'll be sorry!" We were given about twenty minutes to eat, then we marched (I use the word loosely) to the building where physical exams were given. We removed all our clothes, and stood in line waiting for the doctors to arrive. It was mass production in action, led by a doctor and a chief pharmacist's mate. My eyes, ears, nose, throat, heart, lungs, and the lower parts were examined in less than three minutes. Then came two corpsmen armed with an array of needles that were stuck into my arm one after another. Bringing up the rear was a third corpsman who scratched the left biceps with a needle to vaccinate against smallpox. Large signs directed us to the small stores issuing room where we received a canvas sea bag, eight sets of skivvies (tee shirts and boxer shorts), four sets of whites, four sets of dungarees, a black web belt, a white web belt, two brass belt buckles, a pair of tan canvas leggings, two pairs of ankle high shoes ("Boots"), eight pairs of black sox, a dozen white handkerchiefs, four white hats, and a stenciling kit. After stenciling every item except shoes and sox, we donned a set of whites and our boots and leggings, and off we "marched," toting our sea bags on the left shoulder and carrying the handbag containing our civilian clothing in the right hand. We arrived at a rather rundown barracks, one of the many built during the war, a rectangular structure with a flat roof and gray asbestos shingle sidings, two stories high. We were met there by our company "boot pusher," a petty officer first class who was awaiting discharge after four years at war. He was not happy to have this assignment, even though it was temporary, and he showed little interest in teaching or leading.

We wore whites every day, spent many hours on the "grinder," the large drill area in front of the barracks, spent more hours hand scrubbing the barracks deck which badly needed it, and every evening we hand-scrubbed the whites worn that day, cleaning them of the yellow dust from the grinder and the dirt from the deck. The breaks for PT were a welcome diversion for the most part, but some of the tests were a bit difficult, particularly the swimming tests since I had never learned to swim. I received extra instruction in swimming during the first three weeks, and I managed to learn the backstroke, the breast stroke and the crawl, although I never did get the hang of the scissors kick. Endurance in floating and doing the breast stroke were the main things to learn for survival at sea, the former for obvious reasons, and the latter to push oily or flaming water away from you as you swam away from the sinking ship. We also had to swim the length of the pool underwater. Since this required the breast stroke and the frog kick, plus a good set of lungs, I had no difficulty with the underwater test, and in fact went halfway back the length before surfacing, the record for the company.

We were Company 4638, and we began to develop our own sense of esprit despite the lack of interest shown by our boot pusher. He had asked for anyone with a knowledge of close order drill to see him, this on the first day, and four of us did so. I was assigned as platoon leader of the second platoon. The oldest man in our company was Al, who had been a corporal in the New York National Guard, so Al was appointed our company commander. His assistant was another New Yorker, and the first platoon leader was Dick from New Jersey's Admiral Farragut Academy.

The daily drilling on the grinder fell to Dick and me to conduct, each with a platoon of about sixty men, four by fifteen in ranks. Our beloved boot pusher obtained a beach chair with an umbrella, and had it dragged up onto the flat roof, from where he watched us drill, using a pair of Navy binoculars to spot anyone talking in ranks. If he saw some-one talking or fooling around in ranks, and the platoon leader failed to correct it, he would assign extra duty to the platoon leader. Everyone knew this, so just about everyone remained quiet in ranks. About the third week, a short, muscular lad named Rocco was having an argu-ment with the sailor behind him, accusing him of deliberately stepping on his heel. I went back to the two of them and told them to knock it off, which they did, and I thought that was the end of the matter. Our "leader" saw it differently. When I did not turn in report chits on Rocco and the other sailor, I was put on report by our mentor for failing to perform my duty as platoon leader. I was assigned to clean the "grease pits" (galley ranges) that night after evening meal, a chore done in our whites. Our uniforms quickly became so soiled with grease and soot that it would have been impossible to get them white again.

On returning to the barracks that night, dirty and tired, and feeling that there was no justice, I overhead Rocco calling me a sucker for not putting him on report. The next morning, I challenged him to meet me at the gym Saturday for a fight in the ring, to which he reluctantly agreed. Rocco weighed about twenty pounds more than I, and was much more muscular. I lasted two out of the three scheduled rounds, but was unable to answer the bell for the third round, because my face was so battered I could hardly see. Two of my friends took me to the ice cream shop where they got bags of ice and placed them on my face to get the swelling down. Rocco came in and said he was sorry about the whole thing, and we shook hands on that. I later learned that he was a Golden Gloves contender at home. There were no more problems in my platoon.

Boot training was twelve weeks long, and about the sixth week, we were delighted to bid farewell to "Captain Bligh" and to welcome his replacement, a chief gunner's mate from Colorado, who was the salvation of our company. He took us to aircraft and ship recognition classes, to knot tying classes, to boat drills on the Susquehanna River, and spent time in the barracks with us, telling us of his experiences in the war, and teaching us Navy organization and lore from the Bluejackets Manual.

When Graduation Week arrived, he led us to Small Stores and made sure the dress blues we were issued were of the proper fit, and the same for our low-cut dress black shoes. Back at the barracks, he showed us how to roll and tie the black neckerchief. He was an excellent leader, and set an unforgettable example for us. I was named the Honor Man for our company, an award that was never surpassed during my naval career.

Upon completion of two weeks boot leave, I returned to Bainbridge and was placed in the Out-Going Unit, awaiting transfer to Aviation Fundamentals School at Naval Air Station, Jacksonville, Florida. This was to be the low point in my entire naval experience.

Those assigned to OGU were not members of Ship's Company, and therefore, for reasons that still escape me, we were not given base privileges, that is, we were not permitted to leave the OGU area, and when not at our assigned work station, we had to have in our possession our individual work chit, a piece of paper signed by the chief petty officer in charge of our barracks. If an individual was walking in the OGU area and was stopped by the master-at-arms and could not produce his work chit, that individual was reported for being absent from his work station without authorization.

Four of us who were waiting for transfer to Jacksonville were assigned to the gallery scullery where we worked all day cleaning dishes and the metallic trays upon which one was served food. We arrived at the scullery at 0600 after a hasty breakfast at 0530, had a half hour break for noon meal, and worked until 1900, when we ate evening meal and then returned to the barracks. The scullery was under the charge of a seaman second class who was a member of Ship's Company; he was a tyrant if ever there was one. He locked our work chits in the drawer of a wooden desk in his "office," a space off the scullery, and when we were finished for the day, he issued us each a temporary pass that authorized us to proceed from the scullery at 1900, and to return to the scullery at 0530 the following day. Thus, we were in effect restricted to the barracks and the scullery, and could not go to the Exchange, the movies in the evening, or to the club for enlisted. We were initially told that we would only be in OGU for four days, so we figured we could put up with the restriction that long. But on the third day, we were informed that, due to an administrative error, we would not be leaving for another two weeks.

The eighth day in OGU, the Plan of the Day listed the movie for that evening as "Going My Way," with Bing Crosby and Barry Fitzgerald. We decided that we would like to see the movie, so we asked the scullery supervisor if we could have our work chits that evening instead of the temporary passes, explaining that we wanted to go to the movie. He asked why, and we said we wanted to see Bing Crosby, who was a popular crooner of that era. He said, "So you like music and singing?" When we said we did, he said, "Well, let's hear you sing some songs here." He kept us there until well past the time for the movie, and then gave us temporary passes anyway

The next morning, instead of eating breakfast at 0530, we went directly to the scullery, knowing that our master would not arrive until 0700. One of our group knew how to jimmy a lock. He broke into the locked drawer and we took our work chits, shut and locked the drawer, went back to the barracks, changed into clean dungarees, and then went to the football stadium where we took shelter under the stands. Our tyrant was not the brightest light in the world, and had not bothered to find out which barracks we were in, and did not even know our names. We ate at a different mess hall, and since we had our chits, we were safe from the master-at-arms. The third day, a chief boatswain's mate with a grass-cutting work party came upon us, and asked us what we were doing there. When I told him the story of the scullery, he said, "Okay, you're all in my work party now," and we gladly worked for him until our transfers came through. I think it was his example and that of the chief gunner's mate who had taught us so much in boots that kept me positive toward the Navy and my desire to attend the Naval Academy. I had learned that there are both good and bad leaders and that the lessons learned from experience with both were valuable.

The purpose of Aviation Fundamentals School was to give new aviation enlisted men a look at each of the aviation ratings, so that we could make a much more informed choice as to which rating we wanted to learn, and presumably we would be better sailors since we would be working in the rating of our choice. The school lasted ten weeks, during which I became a good friend with Eugene Murphy from Queens, New York. Murph and I had both been in Company 4638 at Bainbridge, so it was natural that we banded together. We both decided that we wanted to be weathermen, the rating for which was aerographer's mate, and the school for which was at the Naval Air Station, Lakehurst, New Jersey.

A half dozen or so of us arrived at Lakehurst from Jacksonville in mid-January of 1947, where we were assigned to the barracks that had been built for the aviation cadets during the war. We were billeted in three-man rooms, a luxury after the open barracks we had occupied at Bainbridge and Jacksonville. We had weekend duty once every four weeks, so the intervening weeks we had liberty from after last class on Friday until 2200 on Sunday. Murph would head for New York and I would head for Baltimore.

About halfway through the school, Murph invited me to come with him to New York, since I had never been there. He arranged dates for us, and after some sightseeing on Saturday, we rode the subway to Manhattan where we picked up our dates. Murph hailed a cab, and when I said I only had forty dollars, he told me not to worry. When he told the cabbie to take us to the Copacabana, I really began to worry. On our arrival at the club, the cabbie told us to forget the fare (we were in our uniforms), and Murph gave me a big smile as if he knew all along that we would not have to pay for the cab. Inside the club, the maitre d' took us to a ringside table where we had a great view of the famous floor show. The dates and I were duly impressed, but I could not stop thinking that the table, the drinks, and the dinner, were going to be the cause of a hefty bill. Murph, on the other hand, clearly had no such concerns, and was enjoying the show as if we were made of money.

Finally, the show was over and the dreaded moment came when the waiter laid a small silver tray on the table and stepped back with an expectant air as he stood there. Murph picked up the check, read it, and without saying a word, handed it to me. Instead of a bill, it held this message: "We hope you enjoyed the evening, and it has been our pleasure to have had you as our guests. /s/ The Management." We looked at the waiter who was smiling now, and when we tried to tip him, he refused. The tables around us applauded as we departed, and our dates were now deeply impressed. We took the uptown subway, dropped off the dates, and went back to Queens. It was a marvelous experience that could only happen in New York City. I asked Murph how he knew that we would not have to pay, and he said he didn't know. Talk about the luck of the Irish!

The school ended in March. Murph was sent to the weather station at Argentia, Newfoundland, and I went to the Navy Hurricane Weather Central at Naval Air Station, Miami, Florida. We would not meet again until 2010.

Duty at the Navy Hurricane Weather Central consisted of standing plotting watches from after morning quarters until 1200, and from 1300 to 1700, four days on, three days off, unless there was a hurricane. In the latter case, we all were either on duty or on call, 24 hours, grabbing food and rest when we could. We were also detailed from time to time to fly in one of the recon planes, the PB4Y-2M, which had been modified to carry four observers who recorded wind, temperature, etc., while the aircraft flew through the hurricane. Locating the eye and sending its latitude and longitude back to Miami was a primary objective of the flight. Sometimes the plane would fly on to Puerto Rico or the Virgin Islands, depending on the location of the storm's eye. On the return flight, the aircraft would again fly into the storm and send the location of the eye to the Center.

During the three days when we did not have the duty, we went out to Miami Beach and spent the day swimming and laying on the beach. I was surprised at the large number of people from New York

City. They were usually very nice to us sailors, and we showed our appreciation by taking them on tours of the Center, which was located at the naval air station at Opalocka, about five miles from Miami.

The aerographers, Navy term for meteorologist, were mostly pilots who needed to get at least four hours of flying time every month to meet the requirements for aviation retention. There were several TBMs (World War II torpedo/bomber) and SB-2Cs (World War II dive bomber) there, and the pilots flew in them for their four hours. They had to have at least one aircrewman with them when they flew, and I flew rear seat in both types of aircraft. The first time I flew in a SB-2C, the pilot said he was going to demonstrate the dive bombing technique he had learned during the war. We flew out to sea, climbing all the while, and when we reached 10,000 feet altitude, he nosed the plane over into a steep dive, and we went screaming down, down, down, all the while I sat looking up at the sky (the rear seater faced aft.). Then came the stunning shock to one's body when the pilot pulled up at about 1500 feet.

The TBM had a large bomb-bay / torpedo bay in which the aviation ordnanceman flew underneath the radioman /gunner who sat on a chair that rotated with the rotation of the gun turret. The occupant of the bomb/torpedo bay could stretch and even walk a bit, but the fumes from the engine were heavy and noxious. Both times I flew in the TBM I was assigned to the bomb/torpedo bay but never could see much while suffering from the fumes. I refused the third invitation to ride a TBM, and the second invitation to enjoy the SB-2C.

In August 1947, having completed the required minimum of one year of active service, I applied for the Naval Academy Preparatory School, then located at Bainbridge, MD. NAPS was intended for the academic preparation of enlisted men who desired to attend the Naval Academy, unlike currently where NAPS is used to prepare young men and women not only from the enlisted ranks but also those high school graduates who are well motivated but are not quite up to the level academically that is considered viable for the Academy.

Upon successful completion of the written screening examination, I received orders to NAPS, and boarded the train for Perryville, MD, arriving there on a sunny morning in September 1947. I was walking toward the station house with my sea bag on my shoulder when I heard a curt voice: "Where are you going, sailor?"

Stopping, I turned around to see a signalman second class with a chest of ribbons and a salty slant to his white hat. "I'm headed for Bainbridge and NAPS."

"Well, so am I, so let's share a cab."

"Fine with me," I replied. Thus began a lifelong friendship with one Frederick Charles Johnson ("Call me Fox Charlie."), from Minnesota and several years at sea in the war in the Pacific. Fox was the senior petty officer in the NAPS student battalion, and readily took to the position of battalion commander.

Bainbridge Naval Training Center was one of the hastily erected training centers built during World War II, and occupied the buildings and campus of Tome School, a private prep school for boys that was struggling to exist when the war started. With the addition of several hundred adjacent farmland acres, the site was soon covered with barracks and school buildings built of gray shingles on two story frame structures, arranged in quadrangles around drill fields, each quadrangle comprising a regiment for recruit training. Yes, it was the same Bainbridge where I had gone through boot training. However, this was to be a far different experience because NAPS was quartered in the buildings and dormitories of the old Tome School, so once again, I was living in a room instead of an open bay barracks. There were four of us in the room, Machinist's Mate 3/c Jean Fitts from Texas, Air Controlman 3/c J. J. Rollins from Bath, New York, Seaman 1/c Jim Johnson from Colorado, and I, Airman 1/c Sagerholm.

The academics at NAPS consisted of a review of algebra, geometry, trigonometry, physics, English, and history. Every one was also required to participate in a sport, either at the varsity, junior varsity, or intramural level. My four years at Baltimore Polytechnic Institute now paid off, both academically and in sports. Having lettered in track and cross country at Poly, I went out for the cross country team, a fall activity, and track in the winter and spring. The academics were not difficult, and I managed to stand second on the final exam, the exam that decided whether or not one was selected for appointment to the Naval Academy. I also lettered in cross country and track, and was interviewed by Tommy Thompson, the track coach at the Academy.

The nine months at NAPS were largely uneventful except for one snowy night in January. All of the officers assigned as instructors were Academy graduates in the rank of ensign through lieutenant, and all were excellent with one exception, an ensign who was sloppy in appearance and obnoxious in manner. This particular night, he had the duty, and so his car was parked outside of Tome Hall, the main building housing the classrooms and the auditorium where the movies were shown at night. It was snowing rather heavily and he failed to notice that the tires on his car were all flat, that is, until he tried to drive the car. Obviously, if all four tires were flat, it was the deliberate act of someone. His reaction was to go to each of the several dormitories (it was now shortly after midnight), roust all of us out of our bunks, and have us form ranks in front of our respective dorms. He then ranted for several minutes about his tires and ended by saying that unless the culprit stepped forward, he would march us through the streets of Bainbridge until the guilty party owned up.

So off we marched in the falling snow, and soon someone started one of the cadence calls, which was immediately taken up by the entire battalion, much to our beloved officer's consternation. Soon, lights were going on in all the officers' quarters, including those of the commanding officer and the executive officer. The latter, Commander (eventually Vice Admiral) William P. Mack, came outside and wanted to know what was going on. When the crestfallen officer lamely explained why we were out there marching in the snow in the dead of night, Commander Mack quietly but firmly ordered him to send us back to our dorms, with the investigation into the cause of the flat tires to commence in the morning.

To my knowledge, the guilty party never was determined, and we were all restricted to the base that weekend. Given our opinion of the victim, we felt the loss of a weekend liberty was worth it.

Halfway through the academic year, I was called into the office of Commander Schmidt, the athletics director. He had been reviewing the records of potential varsity athletes and had noticed the problem with the vision in my right eye. He told me of an ophthalmologist in

Washington, DC, who had developed a course of treatment for astigmatism that corrected the vision in the eye for at least several years. He asked me if I was willing to undergo the treatment, which would require a trip to Washington every Friday afternoon, and I would have to bear the cost. However, he said the doctor gave enlisted men a much reduced rate for the treatment. I jumped at the opportunity, and Commander Schmidt arranged the first appointment. I went there every Friday right up until the end of school, and by that time, the vision in my right eye had improved from 20/30 to 20/20. My belief that somehow I would be able to enter the Academy had been vindicated.

4

The Naval Academy

On 16 June 1948, the appointees from NAPS were discharged from the Navy on board the Reina Mercedes, a former Spanish cruiser that had been captured during the Spanish-American War and was now used as the station ship at the Naval Academy. It contained the Administrative Office as well as providing berthing for enlisted personnel attached to the Academy. We were not permitted to leave the old ship, so we made do with the ship's library and the crew's mess, whiling away the rest of the day. That night, for the first and only time while I was in the Navy, I "slept" in a hammock, trussed up in crew's berthing.

We were rousted out at 0630, donned our sailor uniforms for the last time, and after breakfast, marched over to Memorial Hall to be sworn in as midshipmen. My heart rate was double its normal, or so it seemed, for now I was finally going to realize my long sought-for goal of being a midshipman. As we raised our right hands and took the oath of office, I felt an exhilaration unlike anything I had ever known. At that moment, I felt that I could jump with joy . . . . and I almost did.

By that evening, we had been guided through the barber shop, the uniform shop, and the mess hall, and were now billeted in separate rooms in Bancroft Hall. What a luxury, a room all to myself! However, the very next day, each of us was joined by a newly sworn in midshipman fresh from civilian life, and it was clear that we were expected to show them the basics, such as making up a bunk, shining shoes, squaring away one's locker, keeping the room clean and shipshape, etc. (There was no Induction Day as there is now, where all new midshipmen are sworn in at the same time. We had people arriving throughout the summer, although most had arrived by the end of June. One of my classmates arrived the day before the beginning of academic year, and was totally ignorant of what he was supposed to do; as a result, he missed the first morning's classes, and was not marked missing at muster because his name was not yet on the muster sheet.)

By the third day, enough new mids had arrived to permit the forming of cutter crews, the basic organizational element for Plebe Summer. I don't recall the precise number in a crew, but I think it was nine, eight on the oars and one on the tiller. We were under the general supervision of newly graduated ensigns from the class of 1948B, most of whom frankly were not especially interested in turning the raw material in their hands into red-blooded midshipmen. Fortunately, the slack was taken up by a very senior chief boatswain's mate named Metzger. About five feet five inches tall and about three feet wide, he was appropriately called "Shorty."

What Shorty lacked in height, he more than made up in his strong leadership and salty personality. In short order, he had us stroking away in those whaleboats or cutters, out on the Severn River, and if an oar "caught a crab," Shorty would order "Up oars!" and would patiently repeat the method for all stroking together on the oars, and we would resume the drill. By the middle of the second week, we were becoming proficient to the point where we actually began to enjoy it. This was not to last, however, for having plebes enjoy something was not in the books, so now we moved over to the sailing boats, where we started to learn a new kind of seamanship, the art of sailing, which gave us a good feel for the effects of wind and currents on handling a ship. We still mustered by cutter crews, but were randomly assigned to small sail boats called knockabouts, each with a crew of three or four. They were simple to handle, having only a jib and mainsail, and scooted along handily in a good breeze.

In addition to seamanship, we spent time on the rifle range under the tutelage of Marines, learning the art of marksmanship. It was a welcome addition to our days, but lasted only until we qualified, which took just a week. The Marines then worked with us on the obstacle course, which admittedly was not nearly so difficult as it is now. We spent several hours each week on the course, working to decrease the time to run it.

We also took instruction in Morse code by flashing light, and in memorizing the international signal flags used by all the world's navies. Once we had gained proficiency in signaling, we went back on the Severn River, this time in motor whaleboats, each with an enlisted coxswain on the tiller and an enlisted motor machinist's mate on the engine. Each boat had a signal mast for signal flags, and a small signal light for flashing light drill. Under Shorty's expert guidance, we sailed in formation, executing maneuvers from the Navy signal book, and having a great time, for the most part. Every now and then, a signal would not be properly executed, and then we would have to bring all the boats together in a packed line in order for Shorty to lecture us on the importance of knowing the signals and how to execute the maneuvers signaled since a collision at sea was frowned upon by higher authority.

The summer passed quickly, as did our time to eat and sleep, neither of which ever seemed to be enough. And now, we were approaching the time when the three upper classes would be returning to the Academy. At this time, we learned the companies to which we would be assigned, determined by the foreign language we would be studying. This was dictated by the fact that midshipmen marched to and from classes, made possible by the common curriculum all studied, the single variation being the foreign languages, divided among French, German, Italian, Spanish, Portuguese, and Russian. Spanish and Russian were assigned to the Sixth Battalion. At that time, there were 36 companies in the Brigade, and Companies 31 through 34 were for Spanish language students, while Companies 35 and 36 were for those studying Russian. Jean Fitts, J. J. Rollins and I had been roommates at NAPS and we wished to stay together, so we opted for Spanish, since Fitts and I had both studied Spanish in high school. Thus it was that we were assigned to the 33rd Company, Sixth Battalion, Second Regiment.

For whatever reason, the 33rd Company was a laid-back outfit, with very little of the upper class harassment that went on in other companies. As plebes, we had to double-time when proceeding from one space to another in Bancroft Hall, the huge dormitory that houses the entire Brigade of some 4000 midshipmen, keeping to the outer side of all ladders (stairs), and squaring corners when changing direction. All this was to be done smartly and with eyes "in the boat," that is, straight ahead and level. We were housed in the Sixth Wing of Bancroft Hall, and we soon learned to keep away from the First Regiment area in general, and certain companies in particular, where upper classmen were likely to stop a plebe and give him a hard time over nothing.

After joining the Brigade, we started academic classes as well as PT and organized sports. Every midshipman had to participate in a sport, either varsity, junior varsity, or intramural, the latter being organized by company or battalion, depending upon the sport. Sports competition, marching in weekly parades on Worden Field, and seamanship drills in flashing light and signal flags all counted toward the Company competition for the Colors, awarded at the final parade during June Week, the first week in June when graduation occurred. Since plebes could not participate in varsity or JV sports, those destined for a varsity sport were organized in all-plebe teams, competing against major prep schools and high schools. I had been on the cross-country and track teams at NAPS and I continued in those sports as a plebe.

PT consisted primarily of swimming, which required us to march from the Sixth Wing to the natatorium located in MacDonough Hall, on the far side of Bancroft Hall. We wore our white works over our swim trunks, and marching back to the Sixth Wing with wet trunks under the thin white works was a workout in itself in the winter, but we survived.

My only mishap with upper classmen occurred in the spring of 1949. The tables in King Hall, the large dining facility, were narrow and rectangular, seating two first classmen across the end, with a plebe or two on either side of the firsties, then the third class and the second class, with the arrangement repeated at the other end. This permitted the firsties to quiz the plebes during the meal, and also allowed for the plebes to keep the firsties supplied with food. I never had any problems until I was assigned to the table occupied by Midshipmen Schniebolk and Fishman. Schniebolk was a former enlisted man and was a straight shooter, but his roommate, Fishman, was the spoiled son of a wealthy family from Philadelphia, and could be a bit obnoxious at times.

One Friday evening, Fishman asked me what I thought of Mr. Schniebolk. Since Schniebolk was strict but was a straight shooter, I replied that he was "horses—t." Any answer less than that would have been considered flattery. Schniebolk took it in stride, but then he asked me what I thought of Mr. Fishman. Rather than dance around the answer, I decided to say it as I thought, so I said, "Sir, Mr. Fishman is chickens—t." Everyone laughed except Mr. Fishman and I. Summoning his best imitation of Charles Laughton as Captain Bligh, Fishman ordered me to "Come around after evening meal!" So immediately after evening meal, I chopped to Fishman's room as ordered. Handing me a large dictionary, he ordered me to sit on the "green bench" and read aloud the definition of color, a definition that occupies a good bit of a page and is in fine print. The green bench is non-existent, and sitting on it required one to assume a sitting position with no support, all the while holding a large, heavy dictionary. The next morning, Saturday, I was scheduled to run the quarter-mile and the mile relay against a good team from a prep school. My thighs began to cramp and I knew that if I let the cramps continue, I would not be very useful at the track meet. I noticed that Fishman was not paying much attention to what I was doing, so I stopped reading, stood up, placed the dictionary on the nearby desk, and picking up the imaginary green bench, threw it out the open window. Now both Fishman and Schniebolk were looking at me with puzzled expressions, and Fishman said, "What the hell are you doing?" I replied, "Sir, I just threw the green bench out the window." Fishman was clearly at a loss for words, he simply did not know what to do. Schniebolk burst out laughing, and told me to get the hell out of there, an order with which I immediately complied. Admiral Nelson's injunction to surprise the enemy with the unorthodox had paid off. The next morning, I was informed that Schniebolk had had me assigned to another table.

Plebes were paid the extravagant sum of three dollars in cash each month, we called it our "monthly insult." It was the first Saturday in February, that gray, dreary time in winter known to the mids as the "Dark Ages." There were no more football games to alleviate conditions for the plebes, the only liberty we had being the period between noon meal on Saturday and evening meal formation at 1800. The three dollars was a very heavy weight in my pocket, so after noon meal, I donned my bridge coat (overcoat), and walked out to downtown Annapolis. I wandered into the G. C. Murphy Five and Ten, and there for sale were plastic copies of sub-machine guns, water guns with a capacity of 100 shots. The price was $2.95, and there was no sales tax then. So I plunked down my three bucks, and with a nickel in my pocket, and the gun hidden under my coat, I walked jauntily back to Bancroft Hall, the idea of a fun adventure having formed in my mind.

My brother was a first-classman in the Fourth Battalion, and thus lived in the Second Wing, the wing that fronts onto Tecumseh Court. Whenever he was not escorting a date for the weekend, he and his roommate, George Benas, would turn off the lights, draw the shades, and hit the sack for the afternoon. This was one of those afternoons, so I went into the Second Wing, went into one of the heads, filled up the water gun, went to their room, kicked open the door, switched on the lights, and after announcing "Okay, you guys, this is it!" partially unloaded the water gun through the barrel, thoroughly soaking the two targets.

My brother, bless him, was probably the least athletically inclined midshipman ever to attend the Naval Academy. He was on the sailing team because he sat down while sailing. However, before I could react, he was out of his bunk and across the room, the fastest I had ever seen him move. Grabbing the gun from me, he broke it in half over his knee and then trampled it on the deck. So there was my gun and my $2.95, scraps of plastic amid a pool of water.

"Okay, plebe, chop to your room, get some towels, and get back here to clean up this mess."

"Aye, aye, sir!" and off I went at double-time. It was beginning to sink in on me that I, a lowly plebe, had probably just incurred the wrath of two firsties, never mind that one of them was my brother. So with great trepidation, I returned to their room, and was somewhat reassured on hearing them laughing about the episode. I diligently cleaned up the remains of my water gun, thinking that now I was without cash for the rest of February.

"Now go to your room, and remain there for the rest of the afternoon."

"Aye, aye, sir!" With an inner sigh of relief at the lenient treatment received, I chopped to my room where I saw I had about two hours until evening meal formation. I decided to write my parents, who lived in Baltimore, and tell them the story of the afternoon's water gun episode.

The following Monday afternoon, I was studying in my room when the door opened. It was my brother, who tossed an envelope onto the desk, saying "Mother called and said to give this to you." With that, he was gone. Inside the envelope were three dollar bills.

The class of 1949 graduated on 3 June, and my brother and his fiancée, Anne Monihan, were married that afternoon at St. Mary's Church in Annapolis. I was my brother's best man.

The next morning, half of the class of 1952, including me, together with half of the class of 1950, embarked on an APA, a transport, for the trip down the Chesapeake to Norfolk, Virginia, where we boarded the ships designated for the Midshipman Cruise. I was one of those assigned to the USS Missouri, the battleship which had been the site of the formal surrender of Japan in 1945, ending the Second World War. In addition to Missouri, there were eight destroyers in the task group, the whole being commanded by a rear admiral embarked in Missouri.

The task group got underway early the next morning, our destination being Portsmouth, England. Sophomores at the Naval Academy are officially known as third classmen, but are known in the Brigade as "youngsters," so this cruise was our "Youngster Cruise." Youngster Cruise is intended to give midshipmen a taste of enlisted life, and we were assigned to the ship's various divisions in that capacity. I was assigned to the First Division, the deck division that was responsible for the starboard side of the ship from the forecastle to amidships. We were under the supervision of a boatswain's mate 1/c. The first morning underway, we were at morning quarters on the main deck, starboard side forward. After reading the Plan of the Day to us and giving us general directions as to our duties, he called us to attention, and before dismissing us from quarters, asked if there were any former enlisted men present. Without thinking, I raised my hand, and was then told to see him immediately after quarters.

"So you were an enlisted man?"

"I was an aerographer's mate striker," I informed him.

"Do you know how to use brass polish?"

When I replied in the affirmative, he took me up to the 01 deck, the next deck above the main deck, on the starboard side forward. This was the exact spot where the surrender of Japan had taken place, marked by a round brass plaque embedded in the deck. I was instructed to polish that plaque the very first thing in the morning upon rising at reveille.

At reveille the next morning, I jumped into my dungarees, rushed up to the 01 level, and in short order had the plaque glistening in the sunlight.

After breakfast, all hands were mustered at morning quarters, after which, wash down of all main decks was piped, consisting of wetting the decks with salt water and then scrubbing them with a mixture of sand and saltwater soap, using a stone about six inches square, pushed with a pole that rested in a depression in the top of the stone. These stones were called "holystones." The effect was to make the teak decks bone white. It also caused all nearby items to be splashed with sand and soap, including the plaque I had shined earlier. Not unexpectedly, I was told to shine the plaque again. It occurred to me that the sensible thing to do would be to wait until the holystoning was completed and then shine the plaque, and I so informed the boatswain's mate.

"Look up," he said. "What do you see?"

"I see the flag bridge and the navigation bridge."

"And who do you see standing on those bridges?"

"I see the admiral and the captain."

He pointed down at the plaque and said, "Shine it like I told you."

I used up several cans of brass polish before being transferred to one of the divisions in the Engineering Department.

The ships were at Portsmouth for two weeks, so half of us at a time spent a week in London, and then a week in Portsmouth. While in London, I happened to go into the British Museum, and being in my midshipman uniform, I attracted the attention of an elderly guard. To my delight, he took me to the Nelson room, containing much of the memorabilia of Vice Admiral Lord Nelson, the hero of the battle of Trafalgar, fought in 1802, such as his long glass, his hat and epaulets, etc. There also were some of his hand-written instructions to his captains, as well as some letters to "Dear Emma," his lover, Lady Hamilton. When I returned to Portsmouth, I visited HMS Victory, Nelson's flagship at Trafalgar, preserved in concrete in dry dock in the Navy Yard. Having seen some of Lord Nelson's personal things, and then walking the decks of his ship as he had at Trafalgar, I became a devoted admirer of that great admiral.

For those not familiar with naval history, Nelson's fleet, although slightly out-numbered, defeated the combined fleets of French and Spanish ships in a battle that ended any of Napoleon's intentions to invade Britain, and marked the supreme ascendancy at sea of the Royal Navy for the next hundred years. Unfortunately for Nelson and for Britain, Nelson was mortally wounded during the battle, ending a career marked by bravery, initiative, daring, and innovation.

From Portsmouth, our task group proceeded across the Atlantic to Guantanamo Bay, Cuba, or "Gitmo" as it is known in the fleet. While en route, we were treated to a swim call in the middle of the ocean. It was a strangely exhilarating feeling to be floating in water that was several miles deep.

On arrival at Gitmo, the first thing I did was buy a half gallon of fresh cold milk, and I drank it all in less than five minutes, or so it seemed. My next act was to consume a pint of vanilla ice cream. After two weeks at sea subsisting on the diet served on the Missouri, downing that milk and ice cream was a pure delight. Ice cold Hatuey beer after dinner that night in the Enlisted Men's club was pretty good also. The logo for Hatuey beer is the profile of a Native American, presumably Hatuey. Tradition has it that when Hatuey turns his head and faces you, you have had enough beer. To my knowledge, no one ever has seen Hatuey face to face.

A tragic accident on board Missouri took the life of a midshipman from the class of 1950. The ship was conducting a gunnery exercise off the coast of Cuba, and during an interval while waiting for the tug and target to get on station, the midshipman who was in the rangefinder for the sixteen-inch battery, placed his head down on his arms, forgetting to first lock the heavy rangefinder arm in place. The ship took a roll which caused the arm to swing down onto his head, fracturing his skull and killing him instantly. It was a sad way to end our cruise.

We returned to Norfolk and thence to Annapolis, and the next morning we were on our way for summer leave, with plebe year now well behind us.

Early September of 1949 saw our return to Bancroft Hall and the beginning of Youngster year. It is at this time that each Youngster class first elects class officers, there being no class organization plebe year. My classmate, Jack O'Grady, a close friend from the track squad, nominated me for class president, and for reasons that remain unknown, I was elected.

During Youngster year, the Superintendent, Rear Admiral J. L. Holloway, Jr., was relieved by Vice Admiral Harry W. Hill, who was Superintendent during the remainder of our tour at the Academy. Admiral Hill formed the Brigade Executive Committee, consisting of the three class presidents, Chuck Dobony, class of 1950, Bill Lawrence, class of 1951, and me, class of 1952. We met once a month with the Superintendent, apprising him of our view of things in the Brigade.

As the time approached in the spring of 1950 for final exams, Chuck Dobony spoke to Bill Lawrence and me about his concern regarding a practice known as "passing the gouge," wherein the initial sections in a class to take an exam passed the substance of the exam to the sections taking it later. We all agreed that it was an unethical practice, and eventually could lead to outright cheating. Since there remained only a few weeks before graduation, we agreed that Bill and I would follow up on the issue when we returned in September.

Second class cruise for the class of 1952 consisted of touring various naval aviation and Air Force bases around the country, and was formally called Aviation Indoctrination Tour, but we simply called it Air Cruise. Since there was not yet an Air Force Academy, one-fourth of the graduating classes at West Point and Annapolis served in the Air Force, so one or two Air Force bases were included in the Air Cruise. As usual, the class was split, with half on leave and the other half on cruise. I was in the first Air Cruise group. Our first destination was NAS Grosse Isle, Michigan, flying in transports provided by the Air Force, comfortable aircraft comparable to civilian airliners. During our six days there, we were given introductory hops in several different types of aircraft, and also received ground indoctrination classes in aviation rules for airports and air communications. Grosse Isle is near Detroit, so we toured Ford and General Motors plants, and were entertained at a grand ball in Detroit during our last night in Michigan. I was assigned as escort for Janie Fisher, heiress to the Fisher Auto Body fortune, a very nice young lady whom I never saw again. The date was 24 June 1950.

We returned to our barracks at 0200 or so, and were up at 0500 for the hop to NAS Seattle, our next stop on the cruise. This time, we flew in Marine C-47s, equipped only with bucket seats, not very comfortable for long flights, especially after only three hours of sleep. The flight encountered a lot of rough air, perhaps some of it provided by the Marine Corps, whose representatives seemed to enjoy our misery. We were wearing white works, which were soon soiled and badly wrinkled from the bucket seats and the not too clean interior of the aircraft. We were also all sick from the constant yawing and dipping of the aircraft, so barfing into barf bags was prevalent. We made a refueling stop at Great Falls, Montana, and there we learned of the North Korean invasion of South Korea.

By the time we reached Seattle, we were a mess. When the aircraft landed and stopped, we saw a group of photographers and reporters who had been invited by the Public Affairs Officer of the naval air station to interview us about our reaction to the Korean crisis. However, when the PAO boarded the plane and saw our condition, he immediately turned around, went out, and slammed shut the door. I don't know what he told those reporters, but we were never interviewed.

Subsequent stops included Williams Air Force Base near Phoenix, Arizona, NAS Corpus Christi, NAS Jacksonville, and NAS Floyd Bennett at New York City, flying in the largest amphibious transport plane ever built, the Martin Mars.

One of my classmates who also was in my company, Bob Bell, was from Texas, and had never been to New York. I had told him of my night on the town when I was an enlisted man, and Bob now asked me to show him around the town. It was early evening, and we were in our service dress khaki uniforms, a good looking uniform with its single-breasted blouse and shoulder boards. We started at the lower end of Manhattan, walked around the Battery and Wall Street, and then on up to the area of Fifth Avenue near St. Patrick's Cathedral. Bob was duly impressed with the Gothic beauty of that revered structure. Times Square was a let-down for him, with its glitzy small shops and huge billboards. So I took him down into the subway, and we rode up to the Yorkville section of Manhattan, looking for some good German food in one of the restaurants. As we were walking along, we saw two pretty young women approaching from the opposite direction. Seeing that they had noticed our uniforms, we smiled at them, and receiving smiles in return, we stopped and said hello. It was then that we heard for the first time that particular New York accent that is like no other. It seemed totally out of place for such pretty girls. In fact, we both felt a sense of mild shock. Later in life, every time I heard Archie Bunker and his dear wife speak, I was reminded of our encounter with those girls. But they were very nice, and in response to our question, took us around the corner to a very good German restaurant, where the four of us enjoyed dinner and beer. We parted from them after dinner, and the trip back to Floyd Bennett Field was an uproarious attempt by Bob, with his Texan drawl, trying to imitate the accent of upper Manhattan.

Boarding the Mars once again, we flew the final leg of our aerial odyssey that returned us to the Naval Academy, where we landed on the Severn River. I don't know if the Air Cruise had influenced any of us to go into naval aviation or the Air Force, but it certainly gave us a broad picture of our great nation and the many varied characteristics found among the American populace as well as its equally varied geographical sites and cities.

With the commencement of Second Class year, I was re-elected class president. Bill Lawrence was again elected president of the class of 1951, and a midshipman named Ross Perot was chosen to lead the class of 1953. True to our promise to Chuck Dobony, under the excellent leadership of Bill Lawrence, the three of us tackled the task of rectifying the practice of the "gouge system."

Unlike West Point, the Naval Academy had no institutionalized honor code, although Academy Regulations recognized "honor" offences, such as lying, or cheating, as Class A offences, and those guilty of such were subject to dismissal. It soon became apparent to us that something akin to an honor code was needed. However, our study of West Point's code indicated that there was no room for an honest mistake in judgment or action by a cadet. An act that could be construed as being a violation of the code was acted upon as a violation *ipso facto,* with no apparent leeway for reprieve. We concluded that if justice were to be served, there had to be some provision for remediation when it was a first offense and the circumstances of the case did not clearly show dishonorable intent. The result, after months of work, was creation of the Honor Concept, not an honor code, that required in-depth investigation of the alleged offense, impartial adjudication based upon the results of the investigation, and remediation where warranted. We each presented the proposed Honor Concept to our respective classes, and received unanimous approval. In the process, we cited the "gouge system" as being the initial impetus, and received again unanimous agreement to stop the practice. By the time we had completed the above, graduation for the class of 1951 was drawing near, so, with the concurrence of the Superintendent, it was agreed that implementation would wait until the coming academic year.

For the Second Class, June Week started with the traditional Ring Dance, at which each member of the Second Class received his class ring. With his date, each proceeded into the large replica of a class ring in which stood a binnacle containing water from the seas and oceans of the world. The date had the ring suspended on a ribbon around her neck, and when they entered the replica, she dipped the ring into the waters of the binnacle and then placed it on her midshipman's finger, accompanied by a kiss. This was also a time for midshipmen who were getting engaged to place a miniature of the class ring on the finger of their fiancées, and so I thus became engaged to Peggy Herrlich, the pretty brunette whom I had met at Shure's Drugstore. Naturally, a second kiss, much more meaningful than the first, ensued. The Navy track team had competed against Army that day up at West Point, and the second classmen on the team had then been flown back to Annapolis for the Ring Dance. So I was fairly well bushed, and on that very special evening, I regret to say that I was not a scintillating escort, to say the least, but Peggy was well aware of the day, and took it in stride with affectionate understanding, a trait she showed throughout our marriage.

Once again I was assigned to the first half of First Class Cruise, and once again, I was sailing on USS Missouri. First Class Cruise is designed to let midshipmen work as junior officers, standing Junior Officer of the Deck watch, Assistant Watch Officer in Combat Information Center, or Assistant Engineering Officer of the Watch. Navigation practical works were also part of the cruise, and many an hour was spent taking celestial observations with a sextant and then determining the ship's position.

Our first port of call was Oslo, Norway. The force commander, Rear Admiral James L. Holloway, Jr., our former superintendent, decided to take the route north of Scotland since it was shorter and avoided the busy English Channel. Unfortunately, the seas north of Scotland are frequently beset with weather that is absolutely terrible, with winds of gale force or higher, and resultant seas that are extremely rough, having waves in excess of 40 feet in height. Missouri's main deck was constantly awash, and eventually, all life boats had been swept from their davits.

I was on watch in Flag Plot, the admiral's command center, when the destroyer at the leading edge of the circular screen reported by voice radio that its starboard depth charge rack, located on the starboard quarter just forward of the stern, had been swept clear of its depth charges. Admiral Holloway asked if the charges had been set on safety, as required when not at General Quarters. After a pause, the destroyer captain stated that the maintenance record for the depth charge rack could not be located, and he could not verify the settings on the depth charges, but sufficient time had elapsed for the charges to detonate, and since there had been no explosions, it was presumed the charges were set on Safe. Inasmuch as the destroyer in question was dead ahead of Missouri, there were a few anxious moments in Flag Plot as we waited for the jar of an underwater explosion, but none occurred. The only explosion was an outburst from the admiral when he heard that the maintenance record could not be located. I vowed then and there to ensure that no records for which I was responsible would ever be lost. I also was impressed by the forthright answer that the destroyer captain had given the admiral, with no excuses or any attempt to deflect responsibility.

We were very well treated in Oslo, and all of us were sorry to see our five day stay come to an end. Our next port was Cherbourg, France, where we arrived several days later. Half of us boarded the train for a week in Paris, at the end of which we returned to Cherbourg. Paris was fun and provided some wonderful sites to visit, Notre Dame Cathedral and Napoleon's tomb in Les Invalides, for example, but it was during our week in Cherbourg that my French adventure occurred.

It was July, 1951, and the scars of battle remained on the Carentan Peninsula, so four of us decided to tour the area on bikes that we rented in Cherbourg. We actually were not able to see much since the fields of battle were off-limits due to so much unexploded ordnance, especially mines. Undeterred, we continued on the road to Ste. Mere Eglise, one of the crossroads towns where fierce fighting had occurred. We arrived around noon, and as we entered the village, we noticed a priest entering a small stone church, so we stopped there and went in. Seeing our uniforms and recognizing us as Americans, the priest welcomed us in English, and asked where we were from. At our request, he described what he had seen during the war, and we were shown a cellar where local Jews had been hidden, and later where downed airmen were also hidden until the Underground could get them across the Channel. He said when the people heard that the Allies had landed on the peninsula, there was such joy and elation, a time that no one who experienced it would ever forget. Then came the heavy fighting for several weeks, and much damage was inflicted on the village, but the people accepted it as the price to be paid for liberation. He said that most of the German soldiers whom he encountered were respectful and some even tried to help the villagers get food and other necessities. The Gestapo were the most feared and hated, and were without exception evil men in his opinion. We thanked him and left some money for the church which he gratefully accepted. At his suggestion, we went about a quarter-mile down the road to another crossroads where there was a stone inn. There were large wooden tables in the yard and two elderly women dressed in long black dresses and with white lace scarves around their necks were baking bread in large outdoor stone ovens. The aroma of the bread was especially enticing to four midshipmen who had a considerable appetite from the hours of biking. We sat down at one of the tables, and were served a half-loaf each of piping hot bread just out of the oven, with a large hunk of cheese and a bottle each of red wine. All the other patrons, mostly working men, warmly greeted us and amid shouts of "Bon appetit!" we dug into our bread and cheese with vigor, interspersed by large gulps of the delicious cool wine. The day was rather warm, and our dress blue uniforms added to our thirst. When we left we had finished all the bread, all the cheese, and all the wine. Off we went on our bikes, clearly feeling the effects of the wine, and as we pedaled back toward Cherbourg, we started down a long hill that was a natural invitation for a race. Going as fast as we could, we were neck and neck, four abreast, when as we neared the bottom, out of the left hand side appeared a farmer with a load of hay drawn by two horses, going across the road. It was too late to brake, so we split, with two swerving behind and two crossing ahead of the wagon. The startled horses came to an abrupt stop, nearly tossing the farmer forward from his perch on the front of the wagon. He stood up and was yelling at us while trying to keep the horses under control. We zipped on by, and kept pedaling for all we were worth.

Several hours later, my front tire went flat. I had no choice but to walk the rest of the way back to Cherbourg, pushing the bike as I walked. My colleagues went on ahead to inform the bike shop of my problem, and about 45 minutes later, a small truck appeared and picked me up, together with the bike. I knew that gasoline was still rationed, so I was doubly grateful for their kindness, and left them all the money I had with me, which was not that much, but I hoped it paid for the gas at least.

When I reported back aboard the Missouri, the Officer of the Deck looked at my shoes and rumpled uniform with an expression that did not bode well so I immediately informed him of what had transpired, and was given a reprieve with the direction to get below and get into a clean uniform. Thus ended my French adventure.

The cruise ended with the usual stop at Guantanamo, but this time, for the first time, midshipmen were given liberty in Guantanamo City. The local authorities had arranged for a tea dance at the school gymnasium, where we dutifully reported and began dancing with the young ladies from the area. However, after a while, the mids began slipping out one by one, and by the end of another half hour, the dance was practically deserted, I am sorry to say. It was not one of our shining hours. Several of the first mids to slip out had found the bar area of the town, and were now leading the rest into the dens of wickedness. No one wished to be left behind, and so we gathered like sheep in several adjacent bars, strongly intrigued by the come-ons of the bar girls who somehow knew we were loose in town. I remember sitting at a small round table that was directly under a rotating ceiling fan. I ordered a rum and coke, which was quickly followed by two more, the day being hot and I being thirsty. I recall looking up at the fan and wondering why it had stopped while the room was spinning around underneath it. My alcoholic logic advised me to put my head down on the table while I gripped the table to keep from spinning off of my chair. Some time later, I was awakened by a shore patrolman and told to go out and get into the carry-all that was waiting outside, which I managed to do without incident. There, I joined a half dozen or so classmates, all of us looking a bit worse than we should have, and we sheepishly returned aboard ship. I understand that was also the last time that mids were given liberty in Guantanamo City.

While on cruise, I received a letter from Captain Robert Pirie, the Commandant of Midshipmen, informing me that I had been selected to be the Brigade Captain for the Fall Set. (There were three sets of "stripers," as the midshipmen officers were called, Fall, Winter, and Spring, with the latter being the recognized final rank achieved during first-class year. Whoever was the "six-striper" in the Fall set usually was the Spring or final Brigade Captain.) Upon returning to the Academy after summer leave, I reported to Captain Pirie for instructions as to my duties as commander of the Brigade. Everything was progressing smoothly until he came to Sunday Chapel Service, the Protestant service to which the Brigade marched, less those who were Catholic or Jewish, the latter two groups being sent to their respective services separately and at a different time. By this time, the Academy had a Catholic chaplain in addition to the two Protestant chaplains, so Catholic midshipmen attended Sunday Mass in the chapel at 0700. There being no Jewish chaplain, the Jewish group attended synagogue out in town on Friday evening, and slept in on Sunday. The Protestant service, which was Episcopalian, was attended by all the rest of the Brigade, in dress uniforms, and was enhanced by the participation of the Brigade midshipman officers. Captain Pirie had assumed that I, being of Swedish descent, was Protestant, and he started to tell me of what my duties at the service were. I informed him that I was Catholic, and so could not participate in the Protestant service, information that clearly was upsetting to him. Nevertheless, he understood my position, and said he would brief John Ward, the Brigade deputy commander, who would take my place. Several times, when I was attending some social function on the Yard, I was approached by some of the wives who commented how sad it was to see the six-striper missing from the Sunday service. I had no rejoinder and simply acknowledged their comment. However, it was obvious that there was an underlying dislike if not resentment that suggested that I was being unduly "Roman."

As Fall set six-striper, I had the thrill of leading the Brigade into the football games. There being only small Thompson Field at the Academy then, our major home games were played in Baltimore's Memorial Stadium. Buses took us to Clifton Park in Baltimore, from where we marched the mile or so to the stadium, to the cheers, and sometimes jeers, of the onlookers. When we marched into the stadium, the units and their midshipmen commanders were announced as they entered, giving the rank, name and hometown of each midshipman officer commanding a unit down to the company level. It was a terrific thrill to hear the cheer that went up from the crowd when the announcer named me from Baltimore, a thrill I can never forget.

The Brigade Executive Committee now consisted of me, the re-elected president of my class; Ross Perot, the re-elected president of the class of 1953; and the newly elected president of the class of 1954, Clyde Dean. It was the custom, in line with Navy protocol, for the senior of the three midshipmen to be the group spokesman, with the two junior members speaking only when specifically called on to do so. At our first meeting with Vice Admiral Hill, the Superintendent, in September of 1951, Admiral Hill informed us that he was getting some pressure from the fleet commanders to reinstate the pre-war practice of prohibiting graduates from getting married during the first two years following graduation, to allow them to get their shipboard qualifications done and, at the same time, get some funds in the bank before getting married. He asked us to check with the Brigade as to their reaction to such a proposal. Before I could speak, I being the senior midshipman, Ross Perot stated with considerable force that it was a dumb idea. Admiral Hill looked at Ross, then at me, with a surprised frown on his face, and I told him that we would go back to Bancroft Hall and test the waters among the Brigade, and then I would get back to him. With that, we were excused, and once outside the office, I rather strongly reminded Ross that I was the spokesman, and his outburst was totally out of line. Ross apologized, and I later learned that he had become engaged that summer to a young lady from Goucher College in Baltimore. As it turned out, the whole Brigade thought it was a dumb idea, and the idea was dropped by Admiral Hill.

The Honor Concept having been approved just prior to the graduation of the class of 1951, it was left to the class of 1952 to lead in the implementation of it. Bill Lawrence had provided very strong leadership during our work the previous year in developing the Concept, and it was now up to me to work on the procedures to be followed, a task that involved considerable trial and error, and a great deal of discussion with the Commandant who seemed to have missed the idea of allowing remediation where warranted. It took the entire academic year before a fairly smooth system was in place, and the following year, Ross Perot codified the procedures we had developed during my first class year. With that, the Honor Concept was firmly in place, and still serves the Brigade and the Academy, with some modifications from time to time.

During my tenure as Brigade commander, I stood Midshipman Officer of the Watch duties from time to time in the front office, which included approving chits for medical and dental appointments, among other duties. One afternoon, I approved a chit, and about two minutes after it had been forwarded to the Officer of the Watch, Lieutenant H---, he came rushing into my section of the office with a triumphant leer on his face, and loudly proclaimed that I had not caught an error on the chit, and I was therefore guilty of improper performance of duty, the penalty for which was 15 demerits and three hours of extra duty, or in the case of a striper, restriction for the weekend, requiring reporting every hour to the main office during awake hours less meal times. The error was a discrepancy in the date at the top of the chit and the date for the appointment, they both should have been the same but were one number apart. I did not recall seeing the difference when I checked the chit, but there it was, with a heavy red circle penciled around it. So the following weekend, I dutifully trudged over to the main office and signed the hourly muster report required for those on restriction. Those 15 demerits were more than I had received during the entire three years previously.

In February, 1952, Captain Pirie was relieved as Commandant by Captain Charles Buchanan. The following month, on 15 March, the final set of stripers was announced at the noon meal. Just prior to formation for the noon meal, I was called down to the Commandant's office. As I stood in front of his desk, Captain Buchanan solemnly informed me that I was not going to be the Brigade Captain, nor was I going to be a five or even a four striper, in fact, I was going to be the Sixth Battalion Sub-Commander, a three striper billet. I dutifully acknowledged all this, assuming that my 15 demerits were the cause, although I thought it a bit harsh, but I did not indicate that opinion. Then Captain Buchanan said that I, being the class president, could cause a lot of trouble if I so wished, in retaliation. That comment I found to be insulting, and standing stiffly at attention, I quietly informed Captain Buchanan that I did not come to the Academy to be six-striper, or a five-striper, or any other kind of midshipman striper, and that the only stripe I sought was the ensign's stripe when I graduated, and he need not be concerned that I would seek any kind of retaliation. I then requested permission to be excused, and left to rejoin my company at noon meal formation. There was a buzz of conversation when the six-striper was announced, with my classmates at table with me expressing their disapproval. I told them that I appreciated their support, but asked them to let it go, that the important thing was to graduate and commence our commissioned careers. The next day, I assumed my new duties as battalion deputy, and enjoyed working with Lou Lambert, the battalion four-striper.

With the arrival of the first week of June, we began the series of parades and dances that marked the first four days of June week, to be followed by graduation on Friday morning, the sixth of June. The final parade on Thursday, 5 June, was the Colors Parade, where the company that had amassed the most points during the year-long competition, was awarded the honor of carrying the colors, replete with a pretty girl delivering them from the previous year's colors company to the new colors company. Although we were not aware of it, the Colors Parade would be the last time that Admiral Hill would take the review as Superintendent, his retirement occurring in August.

During Admiral Hill's time as Superintendent, we had seen a steady tightening of discipline with a concurrent reduction in weekend liberties for the upper classes, so that by the time we were first classmen, we had only two weekends during the entire academic year. I was in agreement with the tightening, having seen too many instances of upper classmen neglecting their duties toward the Brigade, their interests seemingly occupied with their plans for weekend liberty. However, there were some of my classmates who felt quite differently about the loss of weekends, most of them in the First Regiment, which ironically had the reputation of being the tighter of the two regiments.

Although I was somewhat aware of their resentment, I had no inkling of any problems resulting there from, nor would I attribute what occurred at the Colors Parade to any widespread resentment among the brigade.

It was now the afternoon of the Colors Parade, and all went according to the rules until it was time for the march in review. The reviewing stand was occupied by Vice Admiral Hill, retired Admiral Louis Denfeld who was a former chief of naval operations and whose cousin was in the class of 1952, Admiral Fechteler, the current chief of naval operations, who was scheduled to make the main address at our graduation, several other four and three star officers, and the secretary of the Navy.

At the order to pass in review, several companies in the First Battalion left their shoes in formation as they marched off. Prank after prank followed, with gloves tossed into the air at the command of "Eyes right!" and similar antics. Standing in front of the Sixth Battalion, the last to march off, the battalion commander and I viewed all this with a great deal of surprise, and Lou, remarking that the pranks were getting a bit out of hand, passed the word back to our ranks that there were to be no such activities by the Sixth Battalion, except for the traditional red lanterns to be carried by the rear rank of the last company. There had been some pranks at the Colors Parades of previous years, but nothing like this, and it seemed to me that the youthful exuberance of some was indeed getting out of hand. I wondered why the stripers in command of the units did not do anything to curb it. That included the brigade commander who I thought should have taken extraordinary measures in view of the extraordinary circumstances.

As we marched past the reviewing stand, we had to dodge not only the stuff left on the field but also the youngsters who were darting around the field, picking up souvenirs.

The next morning at 0600, I was awakened by the Mate of the Deck, informing me that I was to report immediately to the Commandant in his office. I jumped into my white works uniform and chopped down to the office. When I entered I was immediately greeted with "What are you going to do about that disgraceful episode yesterday?" Standing there in dress khakis at rigid attention were the six and five stripers, and I glanced at them to see what they had to say since the parade was the business of the six-striper, not the class president. My attention was rapidly engaged, however, when Captain Buchanan said, "Sagerholm, do you want to graduate?"

"Yes, sir!"

"Well, what are you going to do about this?"

It being apparent that the onus was on me rather than the Brigade Captain, the wheels in my head started spinning, and somehow the thought came to me to make an "impromptu" speech just before I, as class president, led the midshipmen in the traditional three cheers at the graduation, where I would speak of the leadership given us by Admiral Hill (we now knew that he was retiring), mention that the Brigade would remember his example of what it meant to be a solid leader, and wish him well in retirement. Captain Buchanan pondered this proposal for a minute or so, then told me in a very firm tone of voice that I had better make it good!!

I called a meeting of the first class company representatives, told them what was transpiring, and then told them that when I was finished speaking, I would turn to Admiral Hill to shake his hand, at which point they were to ensure that the mids erupted in loud cheers.

Having been a member of the Brigade Executive Committee for the past three years, I had come to know Admiral Hill better than most in the brigade, and I deeply respected him as a leader and a gentleman who was firm but courteous and fair, one who had listened to our comments with due regard. When the time came for me to go up on the stage there in Dahlgren Hall to lead the three cheers "for those we leave behind," I surprised Admiral Hill by speaking at the podium where I began by remarking that we were not the only ones about to leave the hallowed halls of the Academy, that Admiral Hill was also leaving, going into retirement after forty-two years of exemplary service in the Navy. I then praised his leadership and example as Superintendent, and after additional similar comments, all of which I sincerely felt, I wished him and Mrs. Hill, in behalf of the entire Brigade, the traditional fair winds and following seas. I had deep admiration and respect for Admiral Hill, and I meant every word I said.

When I turned to shake his hand, the hall was filled with cheers, as tears ran down the admiral's cheeks. On seeing that, I realized how deeply he had felt the pranks of the day before.

I called for three cheers for those we left behind, we tossed our caps in the air, and finally we had graduated.

PART II.
TO BLUE SEAS

1

The Wedding

St. Mary's Roman Catholic Church, in the Govans section of Baltimore, is built in that lovely and graceful style of Gothic architecture that remains ageless. Its interior in 1952 reflected the traditional Catholic practice of a main altar flanked by two smaller altars in separate alcoves, the left being dedicated to the Blessed Virgin Mary and the right to St. Joseph. Statues of saints were located throughout the church, illuminated by the sun shining through stained glass windows. This was Peggy Herrlich's home parish, and this was where Peggy's mother had insisted that her youngest daughter should be married.

Thus it was, on Saturday, 7 June 1952, that my Best Man, J. J. Rollins, together with other classmates Jean Fitts, Dennis O'Connor, Tom Julian, and Bill Sheehan, all in crisp Navy dress whites, had joined me at ten o'clock at the church for my wedding to Peggy, scheduled for ten-thirty. At ten-twenty-five, the pastor, Monsignor Eckenrode, J. J. and I took our places at the entrance to the sanctuary to await the arrival of the bridal party. Ten-thirty passed and no Peggy was to be seen. At ten-thirty-five, the monsignor whispered to me that if five more minutes elapsed without the bride showing, I would be a free man. I was pondering just how that could affect plans when the doors opened at the front of the church, and there stood a radiant and beautiful Peggy. All thoughts of bachelorhood vanished, and soon Peggy and I were repeating the solemn vows of Holy Matrimony, followed by the Nuptial Mass.

With the final blessing, Peggy and I proceeded down the aisle, through the doors, and under the traditional arch of swords held by my classmates. The waiting limousine took us to the Park Plaza Hotel on Mt. Vernon Place for the reception which, frankly, I have little memory of.

We had bought a used 1948 Plymouth club coupe, and it was waiting for us as we left the reception for Ocean City, MD, for a short honeymoon before taking the trip across the country to my new duty station, the heavy cruiser USS Rochester, home-ported at Long Beach, California. I had changed into service dress khaki and Peggy was wearing a pink suit. As we drove off, Peggy's two brothers-in-law, Keith Kelly and Walt Furlong, wore broad grins and I saw them shaking hands as if congratulating each other. I thought no more of it until we were on the ferry crossing the bay. Peggy asked me to get something out of her suitcase, and when I opened the trunk, I saw only mine. Then it dawned on me what they had done, or rather had not done, namely, they had deliberately failed to load Peggy's suitcase in the car.

As soon as we arrived in Ocean City, we called Peggy's mother, told her of the prank, and she immediately had them take the suitcase to the bus station for delivery to Ocean City the next day. It failed to cause us any concern, Peggy wearing the top of my pajamas, and I the bottom.

After a happy five days in Ocean City, and after a day spent at the wedding of Jean Fitts and Dutch Snyder at which I was Fitts' best man, we packed the car, made our farewells, and headed west on U.S. Route 40.

2

Going West

It was around the middle of June, and I was due at the ship in Long Beach not later than 5 July, so we had about twenty days to travel the several thousand miles to southern California. I planned the trip for an arrival around the first of July to allow time to find a furnished apartment and get settled before reporting aboard. Peggy's uncle Maurice Herrlich, a retired lieutenant commander, and his wife Ethel lived in Long Beach, and they had told Peggy that we could stay with them upon arrival.

The trip was a new experience for both of us, and especially Peggy, since she had never been west before. Although I had flown across the country during my second class cruise, making the trip by car was much different. The vastness of our country was impressive, as was the changing nature of the land and, to a lesser extent, the people. This was prior to the interstate highways that now criss-cross the United States, and the roads invariably passed through the heart of towns and cities, so that we saw much more of our country than does the traveler now who is restricted to the bypasses. We drove through Columbus, Ohio, Indianapolis, Indiana, St. Louis, Missouri, Kansas City, Missouri, Denver, Colorado, Reno, Nevada, San Francisco, Los Angeles, and finally, Long Beach, arriving on 2 July.

At Kansas City, when I was checking into a motel, I was approached by a young man who identified himself as a West Pointer, class of 1950, newly returned from the Korean War, and also newly married. He had seen the Naval Academy sticker on our car, and invited us to join them for some drinks and then dinner in the city. They served up some very good martinis in their motel room, after which we went in our cars, he leading, into town to a very good steak house in the center of the city. Peggy had found the cold martinis to be just what she needed on such a hot day, but as we drove along, the martinis began to take an unexpected effect, and soon she was hanging out the window, laughing and calling out to people we passed, not like her usual self at all. I thought it was funny until we arrived at the restaurant and parked, at which point she fell out of the car when I opened the door for her. Unfazed, she stood up with my help, still giggling, and brushed off her skirt with a sweeping motion of her hand that nearly caused her to again fall. The other couple joined us, and were much amused by Peggy's condition, but then the other bride took Peggy into the ladies room and after several minutes, a much steadier Peggy emerged, still wholly unfazed by it all, and we had a great dinner of Kansas steaks. But Peggy had no more drinks. I never did learn what the Army bride had done to get Peggy rid of the giggles, and Peggy could not remember.

We stayed overnight at Steamboat Springs, Colorado, which was not more than a wide spot in the road, although it had a ski lift, and we took the lift up the mountain and back, getting our photo taken while on it. We also stayed a night in Reno, and it also was not much more than a couple of small casinos where we played some slots and Peggy won about twenty dollars.

Leaving Reno, I decided to detour down into Yosemite, which meant taking some back roads and entering Yosemite from the east. The area is very mountainous, part of the Sierra Nevada range, and the back road I had taken was literally carved out of the side of the mountains, with a long drop on the left side of the road. Peggy was driving while I navigated, but after a bit, she stopped and said she could not drive any farther, the steep drop-off was more than she could handle, just knowing it was there. After about an hour, the road headed west into Yosemite, and the panorama was breath-taking in its beauty. We spent the rest of the morning there, and after lunch, got on the road leading out the west side of the Park. It was a narrow macadam road, rather steep and filled with one S-curve after another. The incoming traffic was heavy, it being a Friday afternoon, and as we headed around a curve I saw a Cadillac driving up the mountain in the middle of the road, the driver repeatedly honking his horn for the cars to get out of his way. There was a steep embankment on the right side of the road, and as I swerved to the right to avoid him, my car went sideways up part of the embankment and then slid back down onto the road, where it collided side-on with the Cadillac. We both stopped, and my car was clearly in the right side of the road, while his was over the dividing stripe and into my side of the road. He climbed out the other side of his car, shouting that he was going to sue me for reckless driving and damaging his car. The driver of the car behind him had a camera, and took a photo of the cars. He then told me that he had been driving behind this idiot for about thirty minutes, and cars had narrowly missed hitting him before I struck his car. My insurance company, USAA, handled the case, and won a total judgment against the other driver, using the photo and statement of the gentleman who had been driving behind him.

When we arrived at Long Beach, we learned that Uncle Maurice was ill, so Aunt Ethel had already found a furnished apartment for us, and we immediately checked in there. At last, we were in our new "home."

3 | USS Rochester (CA-124)

Three new ensigns, namely, Jim Woolway, Joe Denver McCune, and I, reported aboard Rochester the same day, 5 July 1952. Woolway was an Academy classmate while McCune was a product of the NROTC program at the University of Washington. Those ensigns who were commissioned out of Officer Candidate School were several weeks senior to Academy and NROTC graduates, the apparent reasoning in the Bureau of Naval Personnel being that OCS graduates had received their college degrees six months to a year before we had, so they rated being senior. So we ended up being billeted in Boys Town, the name given the nine man bunk room that had three tiers of bunks that wrapped around the barbette of Turret Two.

Rochester, a 17,000 ton heavy cruiser, usually was anchored out in the harbor of Long Beach, thereby saving time for getting underway and tying up when the ship was underway each week for training. She had recently returned from her second deployment to the Korean War, and was entering a four month period of training in preparation for her third deployment. In her previous deployments, she had participated in the landing at Inchon, and in the evacuation of the Marines from Hungnam, and in the process, had gained a reputation for excellence.

I was assigned to the Navigation Division as Assistant Navigator, under Commander Lou Stecher, an Academy graduate, who was due for transfer in a month. The first day underway, Stecher checked my inland waters plotting ability as well as my ability to keep the ship's track up to the minute. When he was satisfied with my performance, he went below to the navigator's cabin, with instructions to call him when we reached the training area off of San Clemente Island. Twenty minutes later, we were approaching the area so I called him and gave him an estimated time of arrival (ETA) of five minutes, and informed him that all was normal. He came up to the bridge, looked at our position on the chart, and said that, while I had kept an accurate track, I had not precisely followed his instructions, which were to call him when we arrived in the area, not five minutes before. This was the first of a number of lessons learned on the job, not the least of them being to first learn the idiosyncracies of the officer for whom you were working. However, not long afterward, CDR Stecher was relieved by LCDR Kuhl, a mustang with an entirely different personality, but this time I made sure to observe his methods and then worked accordingly. (A "mustang" is Navy slang for an officer who has come up through the enlisted ranks, and usually has had no college education, thus is not a "thoroughbred" but instead is a "mustang." It is not a pejorative term, but rather is accorded due respect for the achievement and experience it represents.)

The N Division Officer was Ensign Vic Stamm whose OCS commission predated my Academy commission by about ten days, making him the senior of the two of us. In some similar situations, friction quickly developed, but Vic was a good officer who was easy to work with, and we had no personality conflicts to be bothered with. LCDR Kuhl kept an eye on us but did not interfere as long as we did our work satisfactorily.

All ensigns and those LTJGs who had just come aboard were under the training supervision of the Senior Watch Officer, LT Charles P. Miller, who was also a mustang. LT Miller required each of us to keep a Junior Officer Journal in which we recorded each watch stood and what things we may have learned while on watch. Required qualifications included Junior Officer of the Deck, an underway watch; Quarterdeck Officer of the Watch, an in-port watch; Officer of the Deck (Independent Steaming) and Officer of the Deck (Task Force) . The latter was the top qualification and naturally took the longest to achieve, requiring many hours as JOOD in task force operations, the task force to which we would be attached being TF77, operating off the coast of Korea, usually off the east coast in the Sea of Japan.

Charlie Miller drilled us on TF operations, with emphasis on taking station in the TF formation, using a maneuvering board to calculate course and speed by which to proceed to station. We also learned how to use the TBS radio, the VHF voice radio used for TF rapid bridge-to-bridge communications, particularly for sending maneuvering signals from ATP-1. the Allied Tactical Publication developed for use within NATO. Incidentally, it is popularly believed that TBS stands for Talk-Between-Ships, and it is common to see historians so labeling it. The truth is that TBS just happened to be the BuShips designator for that particular type of radio, with other types having TBR or TBT, etc., designations.

The captain's sea cabin, just aft of the bridge, was where the CO stayed when we were underway, allowing him to quickly reach the bridge if called. The sea cabin contained a compass repeater, a ship's clock, a speed indicator, and a speaker for the TBS radio. Thus the captain could keep on top of maneuvers, a fact that always was in the OOD's mind. The OOD was required to report any ships encountered while we were steaming independently, and to immediately report any significant events occurring on board or within the task force, including change of station. The OOD was also responsible for the entries in the ship's logbook, a handwritten record of each watch and its events, if any, together with the names of the OOD, JOOD, Quartermaster of the Watch (QMOW), and the helmsman. The routine entries of course and speed were made by the QMOW, but the log for a given watch period was signed by the off-going OOD, the final entry for the watch being the time that he was relieved and the name and rank of his relief. It was customary for the mid-watch (midnight to 0400) on New Year's Day to write the log in verse, and some of them were very cleverly done. I never had that task, fortunately, not sure why.

Lookouts were stationed on each wing of the bridge, charged with reporting any ships or aircraft sighted, as well as anything of an unusual nature, including a man overboard. In the latter case, the lookout was trained to keep his binoculars on the man in the water so the OOD could know his location relative to the ship as he maneuvered to make the recovery.

The standard maneuver for recovery of a man overboard is the Williamson turn, where the ship immediately is turned with full rudder toward the side where the man is located. Upon reaching a course ninety degrees left or right of base course, the OOD orders "Shift the rudder" and the ship now starts coming back around to the reciprocal of the base course. This is a relatively quick and safe way to make a recovery since it brings the ship back through the waters it has just traversed, where the man is most likely to be.

In the weeks before deploying to Korea, we drilled and drilled, doing seamanship as well as gunnery exercises. By the time our date to deploy arrived, 1 November 1952, we were ready. Before we reached that level, however, we had some exercises that did not go exactly as intended.

One such exercise remains more vivid than others, probably due to the fact that I was a witness to the event. We were out in the gunnery exercise area, preparing for an anti-aircraft gunnery shoot that called for a plane towing a large sleeve target to make an overhead run, crossing the ship at an angle of 90 degrees. The exercise required the firing ship to have an observer manning binoculars to which was attached a curved scale in degrees. By keeping the binoculars trained on the sleeve, the observer showed the elevation angle of the target on the curved scale, indicated by a small bead that rolled to the low point of the curved scale as the angle of the binoculars increased. The scale was graduated from 0 degrees to 90 degrees. The firing ship was restricted from commencing fire until the scale read 45 degrees, thus ensuring the safety of the tow plane. Firing ceased at an elevation angle of 80 degrees.

We had been on station for well over an hour, and were still waiting to commence an exercise that had been scheduled to start an hour ago. The range had to be cleared of boats and other aircraft, and this had been the principal cause of the delay. Finally, the range was clear, the tow plane and target were on station and ready, and all AA batteries reported ready. LT H..., the assistant gunnery officer, had been tasked with the observer chore, and was standing on the starboard wing of the bridge, with his binoculars trained on the target. He had a special phone talker with him, who was to call out the degrees of elevation, and when 45 degrees was called, LT H… would order "commence firing!" which the phone talker would then pass to all AA batteries.

The plane was told to start its run, and it turned toward us and came in at 90 degrees to our course. LT H… was steadily tracking the target, but there were no calls of target angle of elevation from the phone talker, who was watching the scale on the binoculars. As a result, the target passed over the ship without a shot being fired.

The captain, a tall, muscular Hawaiian named Chillingworth, came storming out onto the wing of the bridge, where he found LT H… staring down at the scale , tapping it with his forefinger.

"What the blankety-blank happened??? Why didn't we fire??"

Without looking up and still tapping the scale, LT H… mumbled something about the bead being stuck, at which point, the captain tore off his cap , threw it on the deck, and stomped on it.

LT H… looked up with an astonished expression, but before he could say anything more, the captain roared at him to get the blankety-blank off the bridge. As JOOD I was standing nearby, and turning to me, the captain, in a quiet, calm voice, told me to assume the observer role and estimate the angle of elevation, using the look-out to train his binoculars on the target. So that's how we completed that particular exercise which was one of the requirements to be done before we could be declared ready to deploy.

Captain Chillingworth was relieved by Captain Richard H. Phillips a week later, and during that week, LT H.. never went above the main deck.

The night before we sailed, I had shipboard duty, so Peggy came out to the ship to have dinner with me in the wardroom. After dinner, we went out onto the main deck, and taking my hand, Peggy led me up to the forecastle. Still holding my hand, she turned to me and said very quietly and in a matter-of-fact tone, "You're going to be a father."

I was totally surprised, and couldn't find any words to say. So she told me that she was going to stay in Long Beach while I was gone, because by the time the ship returned she would be unable to travel, and she was determined to be there when we returned. In full view of the world, I pulled her into my arms and kissed her for a long time, and that said far more than any words ever could.

Peggy left the ship, and that was the last time we were together for the next five months.

4

On the Way to Korea

The ship was steaming at twenty knots in seas of fifteen to twenty feet, causing the bow to shudder up the near side of a wave and then slam down as the bow passed over the crest onto the far side. The combination of pitching up and down and rolling from side to side soon had me sea-sick. I was on the second leg of the dog watch, 1800 to 2000, JOOD on the bridge. The bridge being some forty feet above the waterline caused the roll and pitch to be much greater than down on the lower decks, and I was miserable. This was but the first of many bouts of sea-sickness for me, and it gave me no solace to know that Admiral Nelson of Trafalgar fame also suffered from *mal de mer*. The sight of Diamond Head and Hawaii was doubly beautiful, therefore, and I quickly recovered from my five days of retching.

In November of 1952, Hawaii was still a territory, and the influx of people from the mainland had not yet begun. The cane fields in the lowlands and the pineapple fields in the highlands stretched for miles on Oahu, and except for Waikiki, the beautiful beaches were devoid of people. Four of us rented a jalopy and toured the island, swimming at a quiet beach on the windward side.

After a very quick three days, we were again underway, but this time the seas were not so rough and the ten day passage to Yokosuka, Japan, was filled with drills, junior officer exams for qualifications, and watch-standing.

Following refueling, loading stores and replenishing ammunition at Yokosuka, we were underway for the Sea of Japan via the Strait of Shimonoseki. The next morning, I was called to the bridge where Captain Phillips told me that I was to be his TBS talker whenever he had the conn. We were approaching TF77 that was beginning to appear on the horizon almost dead ahead. The captain had the conn, and rang up flank speed, 25 knots. Combat Information Center reported that the task force consisted of three carriers in a triangular formation on circle 6, with ten destroyers in a circular screen at circle 12. In layman terms, circle 6 meant that the carriers were 6 thousand yards (three nautical miles) from Station Zero, the dead center of the formation, while the escorts were 12 thousand yards from the center. The TF commander, whose call was Jehovah, had ordered Rochester, call Aboveboard, to join the formation and take Station Zero. The task force was on course 180, speed 25 knots, and was conducting flight operations. Our course was 355, speed 25, so we were in effect closing the force at a relative speed of about 50 knots!

Captain Phillips: " Inform Jehovah of our course and speed."

"Aye, aye, sir." On the TBS, "Jehovah, this is Aboveboard. Mike corpen 3-5-5, mike speed 2-5, over."

"This is Jehovah, roger, out."

Captain Phillips: "CIC, report range and bearing to Station Zero."

"Captain, range is about 18,000 yards, closing fast, bearing 351."

Captain Phillips: "Helm, come left to 353."

Helmsman: "Left to 353, aye, sir. Steady 353, sir."

The captain pulled his rather beat-up pipe out of his pocket, and was holding it up in front of his left eye, pipe stem vertical. We passed just astern of the nearest carrier and then he ordered "Left ten degrees rudder."

"Left ten degrees rudder, aye, sir. The rudder is at left ten degrees."

As we gracefully arced to the left, and as our heading was approaching 270, "Left standard rudder."

"Left standard rudder, aye, sir. The rudder is left standard."

"Captain, CIC, station bears 200 and drawing left."

Captain Phillips, "Steady 180."

"Steady 180, aye, sir."

"Captain, CIC, approaching station, on station!"

"Steady on course 180, sir

"Jim, send Jehovah Alfa Station."

"Aye, aye, sir!"

"Jehovah, this is Aboveboard, Alfa Station. Over."

"Aboveboard, this is Jehovah himself. By God, that was a nifty display of seamanship! Well done! Over"

"This is Aboveboard, roger, out."

Without any change in speed, and using what is known as "seaman's eye," Captain Phillips had put us on station in a crisp display of ship handling that could only evoke admiration by all who witnessed it. Considering that it was done before the entire task force, including Vice Admiral Clark, it was a cool maneuver that immediately let all know that Rochester was a smart ship. It took a lot of guts and total self-confidence. (As a commander in charge of a destroyer division at the battle of Surigao Strait, during the landings on Leyte in the Philippines in late October, 1944, he successfully led his destroyers in a night attack against a Japanese force attempting to attack the landings, for which he was awarded the Navy Cross, the Navy's second highest award for bravery.)

5

On the Bomb Line

We were detached the next morning and proceeded to the bomb line off the Kosong peninsula on the east coast of Korea, where we commenced gunfire support missions, firing both 8 inch and 5 inch guns as called for. Nine of us ensigns lived in a bunkroom on the second deck, a room that was wrapped around the barbette of Turret Two. There were three turrets of three 8 inch guns per turret, with two turrets forward on the centerline and the third aft. Each turret rested on a barbette, a large armored cylinder that protected the ammo hoist that delivered 8 inch shells to the turrets from the magazine. Whenever one or more of the guns in Turret Two fired, our room shook so that all the light bulbs were shattered, and the water pipes to our wash basins sprang leaks, requiring the water to be shut off. We also lost the heat from the radiators. The result was a dark, dank room occupied by bodies in bunks, either trying to sleep or using flashlights to read by. Fortunately, there was a head just down the passageway where we could shower and shave, and considering the life endured by our brothers in arms who were on land, we had it good.

I was standing Officer of the Deck watch under instruction, and after a month or so, was qualified as OOD for independent operations, but not for task force ops. We stood four hours on and eight off, with the watch "dogged" every third day, to let all have a fair share of midnight to 0400 watches. Dogging meant that when one stood the watch beginning at 1600, the watch ended at 1800 when the next team came on. This arrangement thus caused a shift in the hours of watches, and also allowed time for the evening meal. Sleep became a luxury, just as it had been at the Academy, with no stretch longer than six hours. The ship had been informed of the possibility of MiGs attacking while we were on the bomb line, so we had dawn and dusk alerts, which meant going to General Quarters, an all hands evolution, of course. No attacks occurred, but we were ready if they had.

When on the bomb line, a ship would replenish about every ten days, taking on fuel from a tanker and food and ammunition from a supply ship. Then we would head up the coast to Wonsan to deliver gun strikes against the large rail yards there. The North Koreans, assisted by the Russians and the Chinese, continually planted mines in the harbor, which had to be swept by our small coastal minesweepers before we could dash into the harbor for our gun strikes. We were provided a chart showing the swept areas, but there was no guarantee that the swept areas were entirely free of mines. Influence mines, that is, mines triggered by noise, or pressure from a passing ship, or a combination of both, as well as mines triggered by a disturbance in the earth's magnetic field, such as that caused by the passage of a steel hull, could have counters that required anywhere from two triggering events to twelve, before the mine would detonate. The complicated task for the minesweepers is thus evident. We went in with the ship at maximum closure, with all watertight doors and hatches dogged shut, so that each man had to remain at his GQ station until we exited the harbor. We entered the harbor at 20 knots and immediately opened fire with our 8 inch guns, to which the enemy replied with 122mm shells. We used our 5 inch mounts for counter-battery fire as well as strikes at targets in the large rail yards. Our rapid response counter-battery fire, and its accuracy, was effective in preventing any hits on Rochester, although from time to time there were some near misses. It was winter, and bitter cold, and those of us on the bridge at GQ were in heavy winter gear as well as flak jackets and helmets. As assistant navigator, my GQ station was the navigation plot on the bridge. My helmet was a shade too large (I never was able to find a liner that fit), and whenever I bent over the chart to plot our position, the helmet slipped forward and down. I had just taken it off when a shell went whizzing by the bridge so close that it shattered one of the windows in the windscreen, showering shards of glass onto the bridge. The captain, who never wore a helmet, only an old cap like that worn by railroad engineers, looked over at me. "Jim, that is no way to get a haircut, get your helmet on."

After 40 days on the bomb line, we were detached and proceeded to Yokosuka for much needed rest, replenishment, and recreation. The officers club at Yokosuka had good food, and entertainment every evening, usually consisting of an orchestra and a singer, so that is where we went for dinner and beers afterward. Commander Dave Armstrong, our Operations Officer, was an Academy graduate, but for some reason, he loved to hear the Illinois alma mater, which he insisted that the junior officers should learn. So every evening, we sang the Illinois alma mater at the bar for Dave, after which he would buy us all a round of beers. The club also had the well-known Japanese "hotsy" baths, where the bather sits in a vertical concrete rectangular tub that is filled with water of about 130 degrees up to the neck. After a few minutes, you feel loose and relaxed, totally enervated. At that point, the water is drained and cold water is thrown onto your head, causing a rapid reinvigoration. With the massage that follows, one leaves totally refreshed.

I spent Christmas Eve of 1952 standing the mid-watch (midnight to 0400) on the bridge. The approach of Christmas made no difference so far as the war was concerned, and we were firing our guns as usual, in response to requests from the Marines on the front lines. The watch passed without incident, and I wearily made my way into our dark and dank bunk room. I walked to my bunk by the light of my flashlight, and when I shone the light on my bunk, there in front of me was a stack of brightly wrapped Christmas presents! My dear Peggy had the foresight and thoughtfulness to buy them, wrap them, and give them to Jim Woolway to hold until Christmas.

6

Saigon

It was the 2nd of January, 1953, and we were back on the bomb line from a gun strike at Wonsan, when the ship received a message from Commander Seventh Fleet, directing us to proceed to Yokosuka at best speed where further orders would follow. The heavy cruiser St. Paul relieved us on the bomb line, and off we went to Yokosuka, with rumors of all kinds buzzing throughout the ship.

As we tied up at our assigned berth in Yokosuka, a number of black cars came driving down the pier, one car of which displayed the flag of Commander Seventh Fleet, Vice Admiral "Jocko" Clark. We hastily assembled side boys as Admiral Clark and a large entourage of uniformed personnel approached the brow to board. Another car arrived with a load of well-dressed civilians who followed Admiral Clark's group. After being piped aboard, Admiral Clark waited on the quarterdeck for the civilians, and once they were aboard, the admiral and the civilians, as well as several officers from the staff, proceeded to the wardroom with our captain, the executive officer, the operations officer, and the navigator. Within about fifteen minutes, Captain Phillips announced that the ship would be getting underway in four hours, and once underway, further announcements would be made to inform us of our mission. Excitement filled the air as the crew worked to refuel and replenish the ship. The rumor mill went into high gear, especially after the arrival of the Fleet band. The lieutenants and warrant officers were not quite so enthralled when the Exec informed them that they were to give up their rooms for the new arrivals. Cots were set up in Sick Bay and a corner of the wardroom for the "displaced persons."

At the appointed time, we got underway, and as we cleared the harbor, the Exec announced on the 1MC intercom that we were sailing to Saigon, the capital of the new Republic of South Vietnam.

I received a call to come to the wardroom, where I was met by the Operations Officer of the Seventh Fleet staff. He handed me a paper on which was a rectangle containing a series of red and yellow stripes, depicting the national ensign of the new republic. He asked me if the signal gang could make that flag, and I assured him that they could. I was directed to make it so, and to inform him when it was ready.

The next day, I took the flag to him for his approval, and received instructions to hold onto the flag and prepare it for "breaking at the fore," the standard procedure followed when rendering honors to a foreign country. Several days later, the band assembled on the main deck where the in-port quarterdeck was located, and I was up on the bridge, standing by to break the flag. As the band struck up the South Vietnamese anthem, I yanked the cord attached to the threads holding the rolled up flag, the flag itself being attached to the halyard on the mast. The flag snapped into the breeze, and all was well.

When we arrived off the mouth of the Saigon River, the ship went to General Quarters for the 46-mile trip up the river to the city of Saigon. We were accompanied by four French gunboats that darted ahead and in and out of the various inlets encountered. The temperature was in the low nineties, degrees Fahrenheit, and with the ship buttoned up for GQ, the interior soon became as hot or hotter than the temperature out on the deck.

We arrived at the harbor of Saigon without incident, and were instructed to proceed up harbor to a soft mud bank on the starboard side, where we ran the bow into the bank. Waiting tugs then pushed the stern upstream, we backed off the mud bank, and headed downstream to our berth at the foot of the main boulevard of Saigon. It was an unusual way to turn the ship around.

We spent five days in Saigon, as I recall, and found it to be an unusual experience as well. By day, all was normal, with the shops open and the streets filled with people, but at sunset, the shops were closed, steel shutters came down over the shop fronts, the streets were empty of people, and as darkness fell, gunfire erupted in various sectors of the city as the Viet Minh came out of hiding and commenced their nightly attacks against the Foreign Legionnaires who were protecting Saigon.

The third day of our visit, a delegation of South Vietnamese officials, dressed in formal cutaway coats and top hats, were met on the quarterdeck by Admiral Clark and the U.S. State Department representatives who had sailed with us. As they crossed the brow onto the quarterdeck, the band struck up their national anthem and I broke the national ensign of South Vietnam. It was a historic moment, we being the first foreign country to render honors to South Vietnam. Eisenhower had been elected president the previous November, and it was at his request that we were now in Saigon, his desire being to show our support for the new republic. It was the very beginning of U.S. involvement in Vietnam.

It was the sixth morning of our stay in Saigon, and the ship was preparing to get underway for the return trip to Japan. The sea detail was set, and I, as assistant navigator, was on the bridge to keep the plot on the chart. The executive officer was standing next to me, receiving the muster reports from the divisions. I heard the phone talker telling him that the First Division was missing a boatswain's mate 2/c. About the same time, the starboard lookout informed the officer of the deck that it appeared a sailor in dress blues was pedaling a pedacycle down the boulevard. Looking out the starboard side, I saw a sailor pedaling a pedacycle. as fast as he could, with a small Vietnamese man in the rickshaw, shouting something in Vietnamese. A pedacycle was a combination bicycle and rickshaw, with the bicycle attached to the rear of the rickshaw. The sailor kept pedaling straight toward the ship, but as he neared the brow, he apparently realized that he could not stop in time to avoid colliding with the end of the brow, so he veered off to his right, and not being able to stop with the weight of the pedacycle, he and the pedacycle, together with the small Vietnamese man, went off the dock into the water. They both were soon pulled out of the water, and dripping wet, he came up to the bridge, accompanied by his division officer. He was the man previously reported as missing.

Obviously unsteady on his feet, he drew himself to attention and saluted the Exec, who was struggling with anger on the one hand and the hilarity of the situation on the other. Finally, the Exec said, "What the hell was that all about?"

"Well, sir," the sailor replied, "I didn't want to miss the ship so I hired a rickshaw to get me here, but the rickshaw guy wouldn't go fast, so I was pedaling as fast as I could, but I couldn't stop because the rickshaw was too heavy and it pulled me into the water."

"Why didn't you just get out of the rickshaw and run? Why were you pedaling it?"

"Well, sir, when I hired the rickshaw, he made me pay him twenty bucks first, so I couldn't leave the rickshaw behind," the sailor replied, with the air of one who was pointing out the obvious.

The Exec was speechless, and when all of us on the bridge burst into laughter, the sailor's division officer took advantage of the circumstances and hustled his man off the bridge. Our arrival had been unusual, and so was our departure.

With Admiral Clark's approval, we made a brief visit to Manila, where Jim Woolway and I were treated to a delightful luncheon at the Manila Country Club, guests of the mother of our Filipino classmate, Alejandro Melchor. Alex was at sea down in the area of Mindanao, so we missed seeing him. Many years later, Alex was the Philippine ambassador to the Soviet Union.

After disembarking Admiral Clark, his staff, and the State Department people in Yokosuka, Japan, we turned to replenishing the ship, and got underway the next morning for our station in the Sea of Japan, providing gunfire support for our Marines who were fighting the Chinese and North Koreans , a tragic waste of lives on both sides while the truce talks went on and on, the North Koreans being stubbornly uncooperative and unyielding in their demands regarding where the cease-fire line should be.

7

California

In mid-March, we left the bomb line for Japan, and then home via Hawaii. We arrived in Long Beach on 6 April 1953, having steamed some 40,000 miles and fired 7,200 rounds of ammunition in support of our forces ashore.

Peggy was there with the rest of the Rochester wives and sweethearts, and was obviously about seven months pregnant. She looked prettier than ever.

After about a week in Long Beach, the ship got underway for the Mare Island Naval Shipyard, at Vallejo, California, on the east shore of San Francisco Bay, north of Oakland. There, the married officers were each billeted in half a Quonset hut, furnished by the Navy. The other half of our hut was occupied by Lieutenant Commander and Mrs. John Rustin, the chief engineer on Rochester. He was a mustang, so they were a relatively older couple, and Mrs. Rustin immediately assumed a motherly role with Peggy and me.

We had been there about two months when, on Friday, 5 June 1953, Captain Phillips was relieved by Captain John Quinn. At the reception afterward, Captain Phillips told Peggy that she should relax and "let that baby come."

The next morning, I was up early because I had the weekend duty aboard the ship, to which I reported at 0745. Shortly before noon, I received a phone call from a nurse at the Mare Island Naval Hospital, informing me that Peggy was in labor, having been brought in by Mrs.

Rustin, and I should get over to the hospital immediately. I explained to the nurse that I had the duty and would have to get permission from the Executive Officer to leave the ship. I soon learned that the Exec was playing golf on the Mare Island course, so it took almost an hour to reach him, and get his permission to go to the hospital.

I arrived sometime after one p.m. and was greeted by a somewhat irate nurse lieutenant, who told me that Peggy had already delivered and I was the father of a baby girl. She took me to Peggy's room, and when I entered, there were several other nurses there, who immediately deposited the baby in my arms. I had never before held a baby, let alone my own baby daughter, and it must have been very apparent since the nurses were laughing and having a grand time watching me. Lisa Marie was born exactly one year after my graduation from the Academy.

Peggy and Lisa had been home, if one could call that half Quonset hut "home," about a month, when the Rustins came over and said that we needed to get out for an evening, and that they would take care of Lisa. It was a Friday, so we went in to San Francisco and went to the Fairmont Hotel's Circus Room, where a pianist entertained the clientele from a piano that was on an elevated, slowly rotating platform in the center of the bar. The pianist also sang, and that was our introduction to a young performer named Nat "King" Cole.

We enjoyed San Francisco, riding the cable cars, shopping in the City of Paris department store, and visiting the shops and restaurants in Ghirardelli Square and along Fisherman's Wharf.

At the end of the summer, we returned to Long Beach, where Peggy and I found a nicely furnished two-bedroom apartment, on the second floor of a three story apartment building in a good section of the city. At Peggy's insistence, we bought a washing machine from Sears, and had Sears install it in the kitchen. The next day, when Peggy did the laundry, the discharge hose came loose and gallons of soapy water cascaded onto the floor and through the ceiling down into the apartment of the owner, a widow in her fifties. She took Sears to small claims court and won a judgment requiring Sears to pay for the repair of the damage. Peggy was elated and thoroughly enjoyed the court scene, especially after being so upset when the incident occurred.

Once in Long Beach, the ship commenced a series of training exercises in the waters between Long Beach and San Diego. I was now the division officer of the Fox Division, the division containing the personnel who manned and maintained the ship's fire control gear, the equipment that directed the gunfire of the main and secondary batteries. There were 54 enlisted, 5 chief petty officers, a chief warrant officer, and two officers, including me. The Assistant Division Officer was Ensign Lou Helvey, an excellent officer.

On 6 December, Jim Woolway and I were promoted to Lieutenant (junior grade). Shortly afterward, Peggy, Lisa and I headed east in Jim's 1952 Chevrolet sedan, which he had graciously swapped with me for our 1948 Plymouth club coupe and the use of our apartment while we were east on Christmas leave. This would be our first trip back since our departure in June of 1952, and it would be the first time my parents and Peggy's mother would see Lisa, who was now six months old.

Since it was winter, I opted for the southernmost highway, US 90 as I recall, crossing from California to Georgia, where we headed north on US 1. It took us about a week, and we arrived at my parents' apartment in Baltimore about nine at night, after driving almost 14 straight hours.

The next days were filled with taking Lisa to all Peggy's relatives and also to her friends, the Little Sisters of the Poor. At the latter, the good nuns took Lisa into the chapel and placed her on the altar in front of the tabernacle, while they knelt and prayed for us. An elderly nun happened to come in at that time, and seeing the baby there on the altar, she at first thought she was seeing an apparition of the Infant Jesus, it being the Christmas season. She uttered a loud, "Oh good Lord!!" but was quickly told that the baby was our Lisa, visiting from California. I don't know of any other babies that have been mistaken for the Baby Jesus.

We returned to Long Beach on 31 December 1953. On 5 January 1954, Rochester got underway for her fourth deployment to the Western Pacific.

8

WestPac II

Rochester was one of three cruisers of the Oregon City class, distinguished from other heavy cruisers by having a single stack instead of the usual two. She displaced 17,000 tons, was 673 feet long and 70 feet in breadth at her widest point. She was armed with nine eight-inch guns in three turrets (two forward and one aft), twelve five-inch guns in six dual mounts, three forward and three aft, and her original 40 mm quad mounts had been replaced with twenty three-inch rapid fire guns in ten dual mounts, five on each side. Propelled by four screws driven by steam, she could make in excess of 30 knots, and at normal cruising speed of 15 knots, she had a range of over 10,000 miles.

Rochester had transferred to the Pacific from the Atlantic in January 1950, and was one of the first US Navy ships to commence operations in the Korean War in June 1950. She took part in every major campaign of the Korean War, and proudly displayed seven stars on her Korean War ribbon. During the war, she was manned by 1448 men and 82 officers, with many of the crew being Reservists who were veterans of World War II. With the signing of the truce in July 1953, these men and officers were released from active duty and returned to civilian life. They were replaced by officers and men in the regular navy, but the numbers manning the ship were now at the normal peacetime level of 1200 men and 75 officers.

After a brief stop at Pearl Harbor, the ship proceeded to Manila, followed by Singapore via a detour to cross the equator just south of Singapore, this to initiate the polliwogs in the crew to the realm of King Neptune where they would earn Shellback status after successfully surviving the rigorous indoctrination that is part of the Crossing the Line ceremony.

Singapore at that time was still part of the British Empire, and we were treated to typical British hospitality, with the first night in port being occupied by a formal reception at the Governor-General's quarters, which of course required us to be in our dress whites. A number of us were invited to a private follow-on reception at the home of a senior member of the British establishment, located on a hill overlooking the harbor. After a few cocktails, I sat down in one of those fan-back wicker chairs, and fell soundly into a deep sleep. Sunlight and chirping birds awakened me, and glancing at my watch, I was shocked to see that it was nearly 0630, and we had morning quarters at 0800. Looking around, I saw that there were a half dozen other officers also stretched out in chairs, sound asleep. I went to each and woke them. About that time, apparently having been awakened by my actions, the host and hostess appeared with an offer of breakfast, but we demurred, citing the need to return to the ship as quickly as possible. Taxis were called, and soon we were on the waterfront, hiring water taxis to ferry us out to the ship that was anchored in the harbor. It was about 0730 when we came alongside Rochester. To our dismay, we heard the 1MC announcing our arrival; now the entire ship knew we had been astray. On reaching the top of the ladder, I saw that my classmate and shipboard roommate, Jim Woolway, was the Officer of the Watch. Jim greeted us with a wide grin, and informed us that morning quarters had been moved up to 0745 to accommodate the captain's schedule, and advised us to get into the uniform of the day, a piece of advice we did not need, and we silently swore to even the score with Woolway. But Jim was such a likeable fellow, one could not stay angry with him, and soon we were laughing with him. We made quarters on time and in uniform, but it was a close run incident.

The following evening, I was assigned to shore patrol duty with a British Marine captain. He knew all of the night spots in town, as well as the bars where sailors were likely to get into trouble. We patrolled throughout the town until 0300, when he dropped me off at the landing to return to the ship. I did not get to sleep until almost 0400, but the evening had been most interesting, and none of Rochester's crew encountered any trouble.

Singapore at that time was a study in contrasts, with wide boulevards occupied by large buildings in the traditional architecture of Britain. But turning a corner, one was likely to find a narrow street filled with people in Indian and Malayan garb, with cots along the side of the street occupied by sleeping males of all ages. I was struck by the lack of females, and remarking on that to the Marine captain, he said that the women were kept inside, since only prostitutes could appear outside without an escort, and certainly no proper female would be sleeping outside. Most of the local shops were apparently owned by Indians, with Chinese operating the remainder. The night life was also a study in contrasts: on the one hand, there were the staid establishments such as the Raffles Hotel, while my Marine friend showed me some establishments that were anything but staid.

Singapore was one of the most interesting and intriguing ports we visited. I have never returned, but if I did, I am sure the city would be far different from my memories of it.

Thailand escaped the wave of colonization that swept into southeast Asia during the 19th century. As a result, the city of Bangkok in 1954 was much as it had been for a long, long time, and accurately reflected the Thai culture with minimal effect from the culture of the West. Steaming from Singapore just five days earlier, we arrived in Bangkok on a bright hot morning, and anchored some distance from the city itself, the channel into the port being too shallow for our ship. The Thai Navy ran a LCI back and forth on a trip that took about four hours one way.

Much of Bangkok was located on klongs, canals that gave the city something of a Venetian atmosphere to our Western eyes. The Navy Club was situated on one of those klongs, and consisted of a one storey building that was completely open on the sides, affording it a pleasant view of the klongs nearby as well as allowing the occasional breeze to provide welcome ventilation.

The first evening in Bangkok, Rochester's wardroom was treated to a sumptuous banquet by the Thai Navy at the Navy Club. We were seated individually in one of those fanback wicker chairs, with a small table at each, and with individual waiters to serve us, one for wine, and one for food. We sat in a long single row, with a Thai officer on either side, and we all faced the klong on which the club was situated. There was an empty space of perhaps fifty feet in width extending the length of our row of seats, and separating us from the klong. In that space, with the klong as background, a troop of Thai ballerinas from the Royal Ballet entertained us with the typical Thai dances, where there is more hand, arm, and neck movement than in a Western ballet, and is totally devoid of the leaps and spins found in the West. The costumes were the classical Thai attire, with a shiny brass head adornment that resembled the pointy spires on their temples, and no shoes or stockings. We were in dress whites with the choker collars, and as the evening progressed, with one course after another accompanied by a different wine for each course, the combination of tight collars, much wine , very spicy food, much wine, a very warm and humid climate, and much wine caused most of us, if not all, to become a bit light-headed. I distinctly remember noting that the dancer in front of my table had several arms extending from each shoulder, each arm moving differently in a waving motion. For some reason, I do not remember anything after that, and have no idea how I came to be on my bunk the next morning, still in my dress whites.

The central part of Bangkok, which I took to be the downtown, was not much like a big city at all, as I recall. There was a block or so consisting of jewelers and silversmiths, sprinkled with some Dutch diamond merchants. There were a few of the ubiquitous Indian merchants, selling tailored goods, and some Chinese money changers. That is my recollection of "downtown" Bangkok. During the war in Vietnam, I understand that Bangkok underwent a major change, not necessarily for the better. Nevertheless, the Bangkok I saw was an exotic city of colorful wats or temples, with multi-colored walls and ringed golden spires, interspersed among the typical Thai open-sided houses and buildings, with the klongs dividing all. Large colorful statues adorned the areas around the wats, giving the effect of a fantasy world inhabited by creatures unknown to us.

Rochester then proceeded to sea for its second visit to Saigon, a visit much different from the first in that now there were no French Foreign Legionnaires, nor were there any French gunboats escorting us on the 46 mile trip up the Saigon River to the city. The settlement of the conflict between the French and the forces of Ho Chi Minh had allowed for the establishment of the Republic of South Vietnam, and the capital city, Saigon, was now bustling with Europeans and Americans, as well as Vietnamese. There were still a number of French businessmen in the city, and their club, the Cercle Sportif, was a popular activity, especially its large swimming pool where the women were already, in 1954, wearing what came to be called bikinis, evidently imported from France. The newly established American embassy held the usual large reception, but had it on board our ship since the embassy was not capable at that time of hosting a large number of guests. The building from which so many escaped in 1975 from Saigon by helicopters lifting them from the rooftop was the same building that housed the embassy in 1954. The new Military Advisory Group was just getting into action and there was an air of optimism and enthusiasm that belied the future.

The remainder of the deployment consisted of exercises at sea with the British Royal Navy, including a landing of Marines at Iwo Jima with Rochester providing simulated gunfire support, and visits to ports in Japan, the Philippines, and a stop at Hong Kong before returning to Long Beach where we arrived on 14 June 1954, having steamed a total of 23,510 miles during our five and a half month cruise.

Lisa was now walking, and delighted in running in the hall of our apartment. But for the first few days after my return, she would stop when she saw me, not sure who that strange man was.

9

The East Coast and Minesweepers

The summer of 1954 saw the first of many moves for the James A. Sagerholm family. As a result of responding to a notice from the Bureau of Naval Personnel, asking for volunteers for mine warfare, I received orders to the Mine Warfare School, located at Yorktown, Virginia. We started across the country once again, and were driving through Texas when Peggy complained of a severe sore throat. I took her to a doctor in Amarillo, and we learned that she had a strep infection. The doctor recommended that she and Lisa fly to Baltimore rather than continuing by auto, since Peggy needed to be resting in bed. So that's what we did. I put them on the flight to Baltimore's Friendship Airport, and notified my parents to meet them.

I continued on Route 66, driving through Arkansas, then up into Missouri, and east on Route 40, arriving in Baltimore four days later. With rest and the good care of my mother, Peggy was doing much better but still needed another week to be back to normal. In the meantime, my father was happily spoiling Lisa with whatever she wanted.

When we arrived at the school in Yorktown to check in, I learned that the nearest available housing was in the Hampton area, near Langley Air Force Base, the housing at Yorktown being reserved for the school staff. We located an apartment that was unfurnished, and immediately went to a furniture store where we bought a bedroom set, a dining set, a couch, and two chairs for the living room, all made of Vermont maple, heavy and rock solid. I still have all but the couch and one of the chairs.

During my tour at the school, the area was hit by a hurricane. The school delayed letting us go home, and as a result, I drove through winds of such force that the windshield became scoured by the blowing sand to the extent that it looked like frosted glass by the time I arrived at Hampton. There were numerous trees down across the roads, but I managed to drive around them, and the fact that I was the only car on the road made it easier to dodge debris. It was either take a chance on driving or spending the night at Yorktown, with Peggy and Lisa in Hampton, so I had no doubts about choosing to drive home.

After completing the six-month course at Mine Warfare School, where I learned the details of every mine then in our inventory, I was sent to the USS Crow (MSC(O)-7), based at the Mine Defense Laboratory in Panama City, Florida. Crow was a coastal minesweeper, displacing 310 tons, with a length of 136 feet and a draft of 9 feet. Built in 1943, she was of wooden construction. Her crew consisted of 4 officers and 32 enlisted men, quite a change for one coming from a heavy cruiser with a crew of 1200. I was the executive officer, the commanding officer was Lieutenant Roger Buck, class of 1950, the engineering officer was Ensign Ed Dudziak, and the minesweeping officer was Ensign Ed Goldstein. There was only one chief petty officer, a Chief Engineman who had nine other engineman ratings under his supervision. There were three cooks, one quartermaster, one signalman, one electronics technician, one electrician, three radiomen, one gunner's mate, three boatswain's mates, and eight seamen. It was the deck force of boatswain's mates and seamen who handled the heavy minesweeping gear.

The ship was equipped with two paravanes, one port and one starboard, that were bullet shaped floats with fins that took the paravanes out away from the ship when they were towed. A heavy cable was attached to the paravane, and to the cable, triangular shaped metal cutters were attached at intervals, so when the cable snagged the cable of a mine, the cutters would cut the mine's cable and the mine then floated to the surface where it was destroyed by the single 40-mm gun mounted on the forecastle. This was the gear used to sweep the mines that are spherical with horns protruding from them. Called contact mines, they are buoyant and are held beneath the water's surface by a cable attached to a box-shaped anchor that sits on the bottom. A ship coming into contact with one of the horns causes the mine to detonate.

There are also mines that lay on the bottom, known as influence mines. Cylindrical in shape, they are activated by a disturbance in the earth's magnetic field caused by the passage of a steel-hulled ship, or by a ship's noise, or by a change in pressure above the mine when a ship passes over it. These mines can also be a combination of any or all of the magnetic, acoustic and pressure activation devices, and can also incorporate counters that are set from one to twelve, so that a minesweeper must activate the same mine up to the counter setting in order to cause the mine to detonate. Requiring sweepers to make multiple passes over the same mine considerably complicates the problem, by increasing the time required to gain a swept channel, and by requiring the minesweeping force to stream magnetic, acoustic and pressure gear.

Mines with magnetic activators are swept by the use of a large electric cable streamed astern of the minesweeper, through which is passed an electric current, creating a disturbance in the magnetic field that simulates that made by a steel-hulled ship. The wooden-hulled minesweeper does not cause a sufficient disturbance to set off the mine, at least that's what we were told.

Acoustic mines are swept by hanging a noise-maker over the side, suspended from a davit. It consists of a streamlined shell containing a heavy steel plate in the front, behind which is a device that strikes the metal plate with a hammer. The acoustic hammer is designed to send sound waves of sufficient magnitude as to cause an acoustic mine to detonate well ahead of the minesweeper. On our hammer's frame, the crew had painted "In God we trust."

Pressure mines pose a difficult problem since the only way to activate the mine is to have a hull pass over it. Clearly, the minesweeper cannot be the activating cause, so some means of towing a hull over the mine is needed in which the towing vehicle is able to avoid the mine.

The Mine Defense Laboratory was tasked to develop and test new equipment and methods for sweeping mines. The difficulty in sweeping pressure-activated mines was one of the challenges faced by the laboratory. The advent at this time of helicopters capable of carrying heavy loads suggested the idea of having a helicopter tow a barge or any sort of disposable hull to sweep pressure mines, thus avoiding the risk of having a minesweeper doing the towing. The laboratory was located on St. Andrews Bay, an arm of the Gulf of Mexico. St. Andrews Bay is a semi-enclosed body of water that is elliptical in shape, with the long axis extending some four miles from shore to shore. To check a helo's ability to tow a ship, it was decided to see how well a helo could tow the Crow.

Crow was stationed at the west end of the bay, and had a heavy cable attached to the forward, starboard cleat and passed through the bullnose in the bow. The lead end of the cable consisted of a bridle of about a foot in diameter, and the cable was extended vertically about fifteen feet above the deck, tended by two deck hands. The helo made a slow and low pass over the bow, hooked the bridle, and commenced towing us across the bay. In less than a minute, we were crossing the bay at a speed of about fifteen knots, heading for the eastern shore which was rapidly looming nearer. The CO called the helo and asked him to stop so we could disconnect, which he did, but the downwash from the helo was making it difficult for our deck hands to unhook the bridle. The ship backed full on both engines, killing our headway, and when I plotted our position, we were less than 500 yards from the shore. We finally managed to unhook, and pronouncing the trial a success, we headed back to the pier at the laboratory. Crow could rightfully claim to be the swiftest coastal minesweeper in the fleet, at least for one day. Subsequent development of this method of sweeping pressure mines employed a large closed cylinder made of heavy steel such that it could withstand the explosion of the mine.

The pier at the laboratory was near an inlet of the bay called Alligator Bayou. There was a copse of scrub pines on a small knoll near the pier, and we set up a small arms firing range there, not far from the water's edge. One night while I was on board as the duty officer, I was out on deck, watching some stray cats catching fish with their paws down at the edge of the water. As I watched, I noticed a barely discernible ripple crossing the still waters of the bayou. The ripple approached the cats and suddenly, two jaws came out of the water, grabbed one of the cats, and disappeared under the water before those cats realized what was happening. I then understood why the bayou had been so named. From then on, we were very careful whenever we used the small arms range.

Several months after our arrival at Panama City, Peggy was again expecting. As the time neared for her to give birth, the ship was informed that we were going to be assigned to Key West temporarily to stand watch over an experimental minefield that was being laid off of Fort Jefferson, south of Key West. This meant that I would not be present at the expected time of delivery. Peggy was under the care of an obstetrician at Tyndall Air Force Base, located outside of Panama City. She mentioned my upcoming absence to the doctor, who suggested that, since she was just a week or so from delivery, he could induce labor prior to our deploying. Peggy and I agreed, and the next day, she entered the hospital.

I was in the waiting room when a nurse came in, obviously upset, and informed me that the act of inducing labor had caused the baby to twist around such that the umbilical cord had wrapped around her neck. An emergency Caesarean operation had been performed, but the baby, a darling little doll of a girl, died just minutes after delivery. It was a tragic moment for us. We buried her in the Catholic Cemetery in Panama City.

Watching that minefield for thirty days was one of the most boring tasks I experienced in the Navy. We were required to remain in the vicinity of the field, constantly patrolling its perimeter to keep fishing boats and any other craft from traversing the field; thus we were unable to conduct any minesweeping exercises that would have been something to fill the time while adding the benefit of useful training. To help morale, the captain scheduled swim call each afternoon, a break that was readily taken by most of the crew.

One afternoon, just after noon meal, and about an hour before swim call, one of the crew was fishing off the fantail and hooked a large fish which he then suspended from one of the davits, with the fish dangling half in the water to keep it fresh until the cooks could get around to dressing it. Within a few minutes, two dorsal fins appeared, heading straight for the fish dangling from the davit. Swiftly striking the fish, the sharks devoured all but its head. There were no more swim calls.

USS Crow being one of just a few Navy vessels stationed in the Gulf of Mexico, we were called upon from time to time to attend events at various cities on the Gulf. We went up the Mississippi to New Orleans for Armed Forces Day, an adventure in itself, dodging the large tree trunks that were encountered every now and then, floating down the river. The good people of New Orleans were most cordial hosts, and we had the run of Bourbon Street, with all dinners and drinks on the house wherever we went, so long as we were in uniform. Our trip down the river was much swifter than the trip going up, with the current in some parts being a good six knots or more.

We also attended the summer festival at St. Simons Island in Georgia. Roger Buck, our skipper, was drafted to be one of the judges at the beauty contest, a chore he undertook with some reluctance, but when I volunteered to take his place, he demurred, citing the call of duty.

After being at New Orleans in the spring and St. Simons Island in the summer, in the following winter we were called to take another heavy task, attending the Mardi Gras at Mobile, Alabama. Not nearly so well known as the Mardi Gras at New Orleans, Mobile's celebration of Fat Tuesday is probably more along the traditional lines of the days when both cities were French possessions. The excessive glitz found in Mardi Gras at New Orleans is absent at Mobile, where the celebration is certainly colorful, but is done with more subdued presentations than New Orleans. As we entered Mobile Bay and passed between the forts on either side of the entrance channel, my imagination was seeing Admiral Farragut and his ships as they passed through these same waters during the Civil War, when Farragut called his ships to battle with his famous exhortation, "Damn the torpedoes!

Captain Drayton, go ahead at full speed!" (He did not say, "Full speed ahead!!" a conceit conceived apparently by a reporter in his account of the battle.) Farragut's principal opponent at Mobile Bay was Confederate Admiral Buchanan, the first superintendent of the Naval Academy, and skipper of CSS Virginia in the battle between the ironclads.

Mobile was the best of the three, due in no small part to my being joined by Peggy at Mobile. We were invited to the banquet held by the oldest of the "crewes," something about magnolias in its name, as I recall. The ladies were all in white evening gowns, including Peggy, and the gentlemen were in cutaways, except for us naval officers, who wore Mess Dress Blues. The banquet was held in the ornate dining room at the home of one of the members of the crewe, whose house was the traditional Southern mansion with white colonnades, situated at the end of a long tree-lined, private road entered through large iron gates. After dinner, served by a number of waiters in white coats, we went to the ballroom where we danced to the music of an orchestra that played waltzes most of the evening. The sight of the ladies in their white gowns, swirling about among the gentlemen in their formal black wear, was something rarely seen, and reminded me of a Hollywood movie in its grandeur.

After sixteen months aboard Crow, I received orders to command USS Rhea (MSC(O)-52), stationed at Charleston, South Carolina. Once more, we were on the move.

10

Charleston and USS Rhea

Charleston sits at the end of a peninsula bounded by the Ashley River on the west and the Cooper River on the east. Charlestonians are fond of saying that Charleston is where the Ashley and the Cooper Rivers meet to form the Atlantic Ocean. However, what those rivers actually form is Charleston harbor, a broad expanse of water, most of which is not navigable due to constant forming and shifting of shoals and sand bars. Fort Sumter, of Civil War fame, sits in the middle of the harbor, to the south of the main ship channel. The channel to the ocean is several miles in length, and with the rivers forming the arms of a Y, the channel forms the leg. Once past the shoreline, it is protected by stone breakwaters on either side, about 100 yards apart. The seaward end of the channel is marked by a sea buoy.

The headquarters of Commander, Mine Force, Atlantic Fleet. ComMinLant for short, was located in a large brick building about a mile up the Ashley River from the harbor, on the Charleston side of the river. It was originally a rice mill, and was still called that by the locals. The minesweepers tied up along the quay in front of the Rice Mill, usually in nests of three or four abreast. The maximum speed of a MSC(O) was about 10.5 knots, and the current in the Ashley River averaged about four knots, except when the electric power company that had dams for hydro-electric power generation well upriver, decided it was time to release some of the dammed water, causing a current of eight knots or so during the passage of the released water.

If a sweeper was assigned a mooring alongside the quay between two nests of other sweepers, and was directed to moor with bow downstream, it was necessary for the ship to go well upstream before turning downstream to approach its mooring place. Then as the mooring site rapidly neared, the ship backed full and if properly handled, came alongside the upstream nest on a heading parallel to the heading of the ships in the nest, and still backing full, swung the stern to port and inside the upstream nest, which cut down much of the current. With the engines still backing and the current now reduced, and with the ship pointing the bow outward from the quay, the resultant vector pushed the ship into its spot alongside the quay. The mooring lines had to be passed to the quay very quickly in order to prevent the ship from drifting down onto the downstream nest when the engines stopped backing. It took skillful ship handling and good teamwork by all, from the engine room to the main deck to the bridge, to make a safe landing. Mooring bow upstream was easier, simply requiring the ship to point the bow toward the quay so as to form an upstream vector across the current's vector such that the resultant vector again pushed the ship into the quay, bow touching first. With the ship held by a line from the bow to the quay, the current then pushed the stern of the ship into the quay. It should have been obvious to the operations people on the staff, who were the ones dictating where we moored, that it was better to have ships stemming the current than backing against it, since more speed was available when going forward as well as better control of the ship. Eventually, the combined voices of the skippers persuaded ComMinLant to let us moor bow upstream.

So why have I bothered to dwell on the above in such detail? Here's why. In making my very first landing after taking command, I adeptly managed to get into the vacant space between two nests of three ships each, only to have the stern line not be properly secured by the seamen on the quay, allowing the ship to drift down on the ship ahead, which had its davit out over the stern, and a hole was punched into the port bow of the Rhea. The ship ahead was in violation of mooring instructions by having its davit swung out over its stern, but I still had a hole in my ship's hull, on my first landing with my new crew. Fortunately, the crew recognized that it was a case of two mishaps not of my doing that caused the puncture both of my ship and of my pride, and they quickly found some heavy plywood and made a decent watertight patch which, when painted over, was hardly noticeable. That took them less than an hour, and when it was finished, I went to the division commander, Lieutenant Commander S., and informed him that I had punched a hole in the port bow while landing the ship, and that the crew had already repaired it. He went down to the ship and inspected the patch, approved it, and told me to ensure it was on our work order for our next maintenance period. Thus began my tour as a commanding officer.

I had assumed command of Rhea in August of 1956, and the following November, Rhea was ordered to undergo an abbreviated overhaul at the civilian shipyard near Elizabeth City, North Carolina. The route to Elizabeth City required transiting north along the coast to the entrance to Chesapeake Bay, thence down the Inland Waterway into Albemarle Sound and up the Elizabeth River to the shipyard., a trip of about two days from Charleston.

The seas around Cape Hatteras can get very rough, and several years previously, a coastal minesweeper had nearly foundered there, being saved by a fleet tug that fortunately happened to be in the vicinity. As a result, ComMinLant required coastal minesweepers that were steaming independently to send a position report every four hours. If a report was not received by one hour past the due time, a sea-air-rescue mission was initiated, which could be an embarrassing experience for the sweeper if it was unable to send its report on time and was otherwise okay. Since the MSC(O)'s were of World War Two vintage, their radar and radios were old and frequently not operating, requiring skippers to resort to other means for sending the posit report within the allotted time. One skipper went to the extent of entering port and making a phone call.

We got underway for Elizabeth City at noon, and as 2000 neared, we were off of Frying Pan Shoals where the Coast Guard maintained a lightship. The radioman informed me that the radio was down, and did not know if it would be operable in time for our 2000 posit report to be sent. I headed toward the lightship, and as we approached, it was evident that no one was on deck. I called for the gunner's mate, and ordered him to fire a clip of rounds from our 40mm gun. The ensuing boom-boom-boom-boom caused the lightship's crew to come running out on deck. I hailed them by megaphone, and asked if we could come alongside. I then asked them to send a message for me, explaining that my radio was inoperable. They readily agreed, and we got our 2000 posit report to Charleston on time.

The next morning, we entered Chesapeake Bay, passed by Norfolk, and turned south into the Inland Waterway, where we embarked a pilot required for that part of the passage. The canal connecting the Chesapeake with Albemarle Sound had signposts like those on rural roads, indicating the direction to take for a specific location. One of our sweeps had followed a sign into a dead end, the sign having been turned by a prankster, so from then on, a pilot was required.

For one accustomed to the open sea, going down the Waterway was a totally different experience. The canal narrowed in width every now and then such that tree branches were scraping along the ship. The depth of water varied also, and there were times when we had less than six feet under the keel. The pilot was in contact with other pilots heading north, and we had to stop several times in a "parking area," a widened spot in the canal, to let north-bound craft pass. Entering Albemarle Sound, we turned west, and then north up the Elizabeth River a short distance to the shipyard.

Elizabeth City is home to a number of fishing craft, most of which were wooden hulls, so the shipyard was suited for repair of our wooden-hulled minesweepers. Wooden hulls become infested with teredos, a slimy worm about six to eight inches long, having a head covered by a hard shell used to bore into the wood, which provides both food and shelter for the worm. Over time, the hull becomes so weakened it must be repaired by removing the outer sheathing and replacing it with new. This was the principal reason for our overhaul, together with repairing the hole in the bow.

We were in a small dry dock, next to the long pier where the fishermen tied up. It was a Friday afternoon, and the boats had all come in for the weekend, laden with their catches. I was standing on deck, watching them unload. When they had finished, I saw some of them gather around a large fire of logs, over which was suspended a large kettle from a tripod. They poured several gallons of milk from a milk can into the kettle, and then tossed in chunks of fresh fish, together with some cut up potatoes. After a bit, the fish chowder was done, its aroma drifting up to my nostrils causing me to lean over the rail. One of the fishermen saw me, and called for me to join them, which I readily did. I had several bowls of the best chowder I have ever tasted, especially enjoying it on that cold winter afternoon. The scene would have made a great Norman Rockwell painting, with the rugged fishermen gathered around the blazing fire and the steaming kettle wafting its aroma into the cold air.

It was now mid-December, and the overhaul being completed, we got underway for the return passage to Charleston, where we would arrive just ten days before Christmas, after an absence of a month or so. All the equipment was in operating condition as a result of repairs made while in the yard, and we entered the Atlantic after an easy transit through the Waterway. We passed Hatteras without incident and the next morning, as we were approaching the sea buoy marking the entrance to Charleston, a heavy blanket of fog was seen moving slowly toward the buoy. It was just shortly after dawn, and soon the sea buoy, some three miles distant, was covered by the fog, However, it was visible on our radar, but when we were about a mile from the buoy, the radar went blank. After checking it, the technician said it would require a part that would take several hours to replace, and when he checked the spares bin, he found that the part was not carried on board and had to be obtained from the tender in Charleston. Our ship to shore radio was working, *mirabile dictu*, so I sent a message to headquarters advising them of our situation and asking when the weather was expected to clear. Back came the reply that fog was expected to persist in our area for the rest of the day.

We were north of the entrance when the fog came in, so I knew we had to go south but I did not know how far. Checking the chart, I saw that the twenty fathom line ran parallel to the coast and intersected the end of the long breakwater that marked the seaward end of the channel. The bridge of the ship was open and was atop the pilothouse, in which was the fathometer, the device that shows the depth of water under the ship. I stationed the executive officer on the fathometer, and taking the conn, I headed the ship toward the shore, marking the depth every half minute as reported by the exec. As we approached the twenty fathom depth, I turned south to run along the twenty fathom line, parallel to the shore. I estimated the visibility to be about 100 yards, sufficient to allow us to sight the breakwater in time for us to turn around its end and enter the channel. After several somewhat anxious minutes there appeared the breakwater through the fog. We went around its end and turned into the channel, hugging the right side in order to keep the breakwater in sight as well as to avoid shipping coming out. By dead reckoning, we were approaching the harbor, and by now were within range of our voice radio, so I called headquarters and asked for the visibility in the harbor. We were told that the fog bank ended at Fort Sumter.

Realizing that I had to be somewhere in the channel to have used voice radio, they called me and asked where we were. At the same time, we broke out of the fog which hung behind us like a great white cotton blanket and there shining in the sun was the harbor and Fort Sumter. Those of the crew who were not on watch had gathered on the forecastle as we worked our way up the channel, and when we broke out of the fog, a loud cheer erupted from the forecastle. I informed headquarters that we had just emerged from the fog and were passing Fort Sumter. They could hear the cheering, and asked me what was going on, and had we repaired the radar. I told them that we had used other means to navigate and would explain upon arrival. The crew often spoke of that occasion, and said that arriving without delay was the best Christmas gift they could have had.

It was early spring, 1957, and the annual Atlantic Fleet exercise was about to begin in the warm and inviting waters of the Caribbean. The Monday that Mine Squadron Four got underway for San Juan, Puerto Rico, was blustery and overcast, with winds of gale force in the forecast.

The squadron, consisting of three divisions of four coastal minesweepers each, was commanded by a captain embarked in USS Pandemus, a World War Two LST that had been converted to be a tender for the minesweepers. One by one, the small wooden ships broke free of the nest in which they had been moored along the quay fronting MinLant headquarters on the Ashley River. Despite the weather, the families of those departing were on the quay, spending those last few precious minutes with husbands and boy friends who would be absent for the next month or so. Giving their loved ones a last minute hug, the sailors and their officers went aboard their ships, and in less than an hour, all thirteen ships were underway and heading down the river toward the channel that would take them to the ocean. Pandemus was leading the long column, and as they passed Fort Sumter, the park ranger there dipped the colors floating over the fort, answered one by one by the ships as each passed the fort. It was not the practice for the fort to do so, but this obviously was a special occasion warranting a special salute.

An hour later, all ships of the squadron had cleared the channel and were past the sea buoy. It was now time to form up for the transit to San Juan, and the signal came by voice radio from Pandemus for the ships to take station in a circular formation on circle six, with Pandemus the formation guide in station zero. Translation: the ships formed a circle with Pandemus in the center at a distance of six thousand yards, or three nautical miles, in radius.

The high winds lashed the sea, and waves of ten feet or so were already being encountered. Green water crashed over the bow, and streamed down the main deck, making it very difficult for the crew assigned to the open bridge from where the ship was conned to ascend from below or descend when going off watch. All topside watch standers were in foul weather gear, rubber coats and boots, and some wore the sou'wester hats one sees so often in drawings of seamen. Formation speed was seven knots, and with a top speed of 10.5 knots, the small ships took several hours, fighting the wind and seas, to gain their respective stations in the circular screen.

As night approached, the order was received to steam at darkened ship, meaning no lights were permitted topside except for the running lights, green to starboard and red to port, with a single white masthead light centered above them, and a white stern light showing aft. Ships maintained station by observing the radar scope for the surface search radar which was in the pilot house under the open bridge. The radar was manned by one of the three radarmen in the crew, who reported range and bearing to the guide every five minutes. The radar was the original set that had been provided to the ship in 1945, and it was notoriously unreliable, prone to breakdowns at any time for no apparent reason, breakdowns which seemed to occur whenever the radar was needed for navigation or, in this case, for station keeping. However, our radar on Rhea performed without any hitches for the entire period we were gone, a minor miracle.

The next day at sea saw no letup in the weather, and the water crashing down the main deck had broken the ports on the starboard side of the galley, flooding the galley and causing the galley ranges to become inoperable, so we were reduced to eating cold soggy sandwiches, but the coffee maker was intact, and we at least had hot coffee to go with our sandwiches. With the constant plunging up and down, accompanied by heavy rolls to either side, no one seemd to be particularly hungry anyway, so the lack of a hot meal was not of particular concern.

What was of concern was the fear of getting water into the engine room, which was a large open bay amidships, covered with a fidley deck, a raised structure some four feet higher than the main deck. Water in that critical space could cause the engines to shut down, and worse, could short the electric generators that powered the ship's equipment. At least one minesweeper had managed to barely survive when its fidley deck shifted in heavy seas and the engine room was flooded. With all power gone and unable to make headway, the ship was foundering when it was rescued by a fleet tug that luckily was in the vicinity. We were in the storm for the entire voyage, and the fact that no one's engine room was flooded was another minor miracle.

The third night underway, at about 2100, the ship in the station ahead of us suddenly turned on all its deck lights, and simultaneously reported by voice radio that their quartermaster of the watch had been swept off the ladder by which one climbed up to the bridge. For some reason, he had taken the ladder on the weather side rather than the one on the lee side, and a large wave washed him into the sea. The ship was the Hornbill, commanded by an Academy classmate of mine. He immediately hauled out of formation, and turned to starboard, which meant that he would be approaching our position.

I ordered all our lights to be turned on, and altered course to port to avoid Hornbill. At that instant , the squadron commodore ordered our mine division, of which Hornbill was a part, to leave the formation and conduct a sweep of the area where the lad had been lost overboard. We formed a search line, and were shortly thereafter joined by a second division, who formed up on our line abreast, so there were now eight ships slowly combing the area, sweeping back and forth. After several hours of fruitless search, the commodore called off the search and we returned to our respective stations. The cruel sea had clamed another sailor for Davey Jones' Locker.

The sight of the large stone fortress that guards the entrance to San Juan harbor was a welcome sight indeed, after a week of continual battering by the wind and sea. After tying up alongside the quay in the harbor, we enjoyed a few minutes of motionless relaxation. Then the word came down to have all COs assemble in the wardroom of Pandemus. Stepping ashore, for the first minute or so while walking down the quay, I experienced the sensation of the ground rocking under my feet, causing me to walk with the unsteady gait of a drunk. This was the first and only time I encountered the phenomenon known as "sea legs."

Each sweeper had been assigned an area for independent operational training, the whole being in the vicinity of Puerto Rico and the Virgin Islands. After a day's rest in port, we got underway and spent the day in our area streaming our gear and making any required repairs resulting from the storm. With our galley ports once again intact, we were in good condition.

As evening neared, I checked the charts for a sheltered area where we could anchor for the night, in order to conserve fuel and to give the crew additional rest. I noticed that the islands of St. Thomas and St. John, part of the Virgin Islands, formed a sheltered bay labeled Caneel Bay on the chart. We arrived in the bay at sunset, and anchored in water so clear we could see the anchor on the bottom, at a depth of about forty feet.

I had just sat down in the small wardroom when the watch informed me that we were getting a flashing light message from the shore. I went on deck, and could see a flashing light, sending Morse code, coming from a cluster of small buildings on St. John Island. I caught the last part of the message, ..."on the house." Our one and only signalman, a petty officer first class, had been copying the message, and when he gave it to me, it read: "Minesweeper 52, welcome to Caneel Bay and Caneel Bay Plantation, the newest resort in the Virgin Islands. Come over and enjoy a drink on the house." Our signalman informed me that the sender had identified himself as a former signalman who was now the manager of the club at Caneel Bay Plantation.

Our only boat was a punt that could accommodate about four people, driven by a small outboard engine. We swung the punt out into the water, and began ferrying the liberty party, three at a time plus the duty crewman operating the punt, an evolution that took about an hour. I went over in the last run, and instructed the punt operator to return in an hour to begin the return runs for the liberty party.

I was met at the pier by the manager who had invited us over, and we went up to the club, where we were greeted by a number of the guests who were enjoying having our young sailors among them. The manager told me that what had been an abandoned sugar plantation had been converted by Laurence Rockefeller and his wife, Mary, into a different kind of resort, where the guests lived in the restored old buildings of the plantation, including the slave quarters. All were of masonry construction and all were painted a subdued pink that made a pleasant contrast with the green foliage of palms and bushes. Much of the funds for the restoration had been provided by the Rockefeller Foundation.

After a very pleasant evening, conversing with the guests and having a rum maitai drink, we returned to Rhea, where I asked for volunteers from the liberty party who were willing to relieve the watch so they could also share in the evening ashore. By midnight, all were back aboard, and the crew was congratulating our luck in having anchored in Caneel Bay, a very good way to begin our participation in Operation Springboard.

After a week of independent operations, we rendezvoused with the rest of our division, which then joined with the rest of the squadron. Four Australian ocean minesweepers also joined us, this to be their last operation with the Atlantic Fleet before commencing their long voyage home.

We spent the next four days sweeping a minefield and escorting destroyers and other combatant ships through the swept channel within the minefield. The work was demanding but we felt satisfied that we had accomplished our mission, and we were at peak readiness as a mine force.

The last day of the exercise, we steamed into the harbor at St. Thomas, the most developed of the Virgin Islands. That evening, the mine force enjoyed a farewell gathering at Blackbeard's Inn, located up in the heights above the town of St. Thomas. Our Australian comrades joined us there, and gave visible proof of the exceptional capacity of Australian sailors to consume alcohol and remain in command of their faculties.

The voyage home was far different from the trip to the Caribbean, with gentle winds and seas, so that we arrived in Charleston in good condition, ready to be once again with our families and friends.

Shortly after our return, I received orders to the Naval Intelligence School as a student, an assignment I had requested, work in intelligence having appealed to me as something interesting to do when on shore duty. The school was located in Anacostia, District of Columbia, so we were slated for another move in August.

In the meantime, we were blessed with the arrival on 10 May, 1957, of our daughter, Ann Denise, delivered by C-section at Charleston Naval Hospital. Mother and newborn both did well, and were home three days later. Lisa now had a sister, whom she greeted with less than enthusiasm after four years of being the only child. Later on when they were older, Lisa readily took to the role of big sister for her younger siblings.

11

Shore Duty

The class at Naval Intelligence School consisted of some thirty lieutenants and lieutenant commanders, a mixture of line officers who
remained line and those who converted to intelligence specialty officers. One of the latter was a lieutenant named Bob Inman, with
whom I formed a lifelong friendship, and who eventually rose to
four star rank at the highest levels of national intelligence, a highly
respected officer of exceptional intelligence and keenly astute perception of world affairs.

The curriculum included not only the techniques one needed to
learn but also a comprehensive course in international affairs. The former provided some of the lighter moments in the nine month course.
One of the techniques was the art of tailing a target. It took a three
man team to keep the target under surveillance without hopefully
being detected by him. We were assigned a field exercise where we
were given a photo of the target, and were told that he was expected
to arrive by train at Union Station at around nine in the morning. Our
task was to follow him until his departure by train that afternoon and
report where he went and what he did.

We took up position in the station near where the train would
arrive, and sure enough, there he was, getting off one of the cars. He
hailed a cab, and just like in the movies, we hailed one also and told
the driver to follow that cab, but not too closely. Our driver found the
chase exciting, he apparently assuming that we were FBI or CIA. Our

man got out in front of Woodward and Lothrop's department store in downtown Washington, we doing the same farther down the street. We paid our driver, and told him not to discuss our trip with anyone, and he solemnly assured us that he would not.

When we entered the store, our target was just getting on one of the elevators. We hurried over and split our team, one man to board the up elevator and work his way down until he spotted our man, and the other two taking station outside the elevators in case he came down before our accomplice gained tail on him. The elevator arrived, the door opened, and people were departing while others were entering it. As our man entered, there was our target, getting off. Our man had no choice but to go up one floor and then get off, and race down the stairs. In the meantime, we had to keep the target in sight and hope that our man could make it back down before we moved out of sight of anyone near the elevators and the stairs. This was well before cell phones came, but walkie-talkie radios, developed during World War Two, were on the market, and we were equipped with them. They were fairly bulky, and using one was unavoidably noticeable, which precluded their use in the crowded store. Our target went outside as soon as he reached the door, so the two of us followed, one on each side of the street. He went into a small restaurant and sat down at a table next to the large window looking out onto the street. The restaurant was on my side of the street so I went in to see what he did or whom he met. No sooner had I sat down at the counter than he got up and quickly walked out the door. I had been recognized by him as a tailer, so I stayed in the restaurant, having a donut and coffee, trusting that our outside man would continue the trail. He had been joined by our team member who had been left in the department store. I glanced out the large window and saw our target standing across the street, camera in hand, taking a photo of the restaurant. I also saw our two guys walking down the street, one on each side. They both slowed and then stopped, a giveaway to an experienced agent that he was being followed by the men who had stopped.

We turned in our report the next day, and were in turn treated to our photos that had been taken by our target. We got a C for our efforts since we had been able to provide a detailed account of the target's activities, but we knew if we had been in a real surveillance mission, we would have been declared *persona non grata* by whatever country we were working in.

Our same team had better luck on our next field exercise. This time, we were assigned the task of driving to Baltimore to take photos of the commercial harbor of that city. The directions given us called for us to proceed to an old cemetery in east Baltimore, on a hill overlooking the harbor. Photos were to be taken of any ships that were in port, photography being a basic tool of intelligence operatives. We were issued cameras, and were expected to do our own developing of the film.

As we were driving on the highway to Baltimore, we were passed by a car traveling at a speed well in excess of the legal limit. One of our team recognized the driver as the man we had trailed several weeks earlier in Washington.

Suspecting that he had recognized us and thus would have made a mental note of our car, I suggested that we proceed to another site from which to take our photos. The others agreed, and we drove wide of the cemetery and found a vacant lot several blocks down the street from the cemetery, at nearly the same elevation and essentially the same views of the harbor.

Thus we totally avoided the counter-agent and this time received an A. Our photos were judged the best of any team, and we were the only team that escaped detection.

Having completed the course in June of 1958, I was assigned to the Office of Naval Intelligence, headquartered in the Pentagon, and was placed in charge of the Latin America desk since I had taken Spanish at the Academy. I worked alongside three civilians who each held doctorates in history.

Our principal focus was on Cuba, where rebel forces, led by a young Cuban named Fidel Castro, were fighting the forces of President Fulgencio Batista in the mountains of eastern Cuba. We were receiving reports from several Cuban sources that Castro and his second in command, Che Guevara, an Argentine, were Communists, although Castro proclaimed he and his followers were simply Cuban patriots who were seeking to oust the corrupt Batista regime and give Cuba a decent government.

The Congress and the Eisenhower administration, as well as the majority of Americans, supported Castro, eager to see the corrupt and dictatorial Batista rule ended. However, the Navy in the person of the Chief of Naval Operations, Admiral Arleigh Burke, on the basis of our reports, warned the Department of Defense that there was growing evidence that Castro was indeed a Communist who intended to establish a Communist government in Cuba, once Batista had been ousted.

Despite Admiral Burke's warnings, the U.S. government continued to support Castro, convinced that he was a force for the better in Cuba.

The day after Christmas while I was on leave, I was notified by the Washington area detailer in the Bureau of Naval Personnel that I was to report to the Pentagon the following week to be interviewed by Vice Admiral H. D. Riley, for possible assignment as his flag lieutenant. Admiral Riley was Chief of Staff, Pacific Command, headquartered in Hawaii.

During the past eighteen months or so, I had been wearing civilian clothing, that being the custom in Washington. However, for the interview with Admiral Riley, I was told to be in uniform. Unfortunately, the gold braid on the sleeves that denoted my rank, consisting of two stripes topped by the star indicating I was a line officer as opposed to a staff corps officer, had become badly tarnished and needed to be replaced. When I called the Naval Uniform Shop, I was told that they could furnish the braid and stars, but the seamstress was on Christmas leave and would not return until after the first of January. So I bought the braid and stars and my dear wife hand-stitched the new stripes and stars onto the sleeves of my dress blues.

On the appointed day, I went to the Pentagon where I proceeded to the office for visiting flag officers, located on the E Ring in the Navy section. When I entered the outer office, I was met by Lieutenant Commander Stansfield Turner, Admiral Riley's Executive Assistant, and two other nominee lieutenants. I was the last to be interviewed, and met briefly with the admiral, who asked a few questions about my prior experience and qualifications and then dismissed me. After a few moments, Turner came out and told us that I had been selected, and he told the others they could go, but I was to stay for instructions from Turner as to when I was to report to Hawaii.

I was a bit shocked when Stan Turner told me that I was to be in Riley's office in one week. I explained that we had bought a house in Falls Church, Virginia, expecting to be in the Washington area for three years, and that I would need some time, say a month, to sell it and arrange the trip to Hawaii for my family. Stan said the admiral needed me there next week, and that I would have to be there then, leaving Peggy to wrap up affairs in Falls Church.

A week later, I boarded a TWA flight out of National Airport, and landed in San Francisco eight hours later. After several days in San Francisco, I was placed on an Air Force transport from Oakland to Honolulu, landing at Hickam Air Force Base ten hours later. For the next month, I lived in the bachelor officers quarters at the Pearl harbor Naval Base. CincPac headquarters was at Aiea Heights, overlooking Pearl Harbor. Each morning, a staff car driven by a Marine corporal picked up Admiral Riley at his quarters in Makalapa, a section of the Pearl Harbor complex. Since I did not have a car, the driver picked me up first, and then we stopped for the admiral. It gave him a chance to chat informally with me before we arrived at the office, and I learned that he, a naval aviator, had commanded the carrier Coral Sea as a captain, that he had at one point been the pilot for President Franklin Roosevelt, and that he was divorced and had a teen-age daughter, Lynne, who was a student at Punahou, a private school in Honolulu.

Working in the office of the number two admiral at the Pacific Command headquarters was a valuable learning experience, especially working with Stan Turner, a Rhodes Scholar from the Naval Academy class of 1947. I quickly became familiar with the various projects being pursued by the Pacific Command, headed by Admiral Don Felt, a tough four star naval aviator who had been the Vice Chief of Naval Operations, and was a close confidant of Admiral Burke with whom he communicated regularly on not only Pacific affairs but a variety of subjects regarding the Navy in general.

Admiral Felt considered any officer on the staff, including the various aides, to be available for his use, and thus it was that I was summoned to his office on a Wednesday afternoon and was told to go fetch the general commanding the Air Force component of the Pacific Command for an emergency meeting of the component commanders in Felt's office.

The Communist government of China was shelling the offshore islands of Quemoy and Matsu, held by the forces of Chiang-Kai-Shek, and the United States, bound by treaty to defend Taiwan and the Nationalist government there headed by Chiang, was being pressed by Taiwan to protect Quemoy and Matsu as well, the argument being that they served as picket outposts in the defense of Taiwan.

I rounded up Admiral Felt's driver and car, and off we headed for Hickam and CincPacAF headquarters, where I confirmed that they had refused to interrupt the general's golf game, played once a week on Wednesday afternoon. I commandeered a golf cart, and took off down the cart path. I finally found the general preparing to tee off on the eleventh tee. I briefly gave him the picture and he immediately agreed to go in his golfing togs, and in short order we delivered him to the meeting.

The United States made clear to China that we intended to defend Taiwan and all its outlying possessions, and the crisis was resolved without any further gunfire.

A month or so after I arrived in Hawaii, Peggy and our three children (Jeannine had been born at Bethesda Naval Hospital on 15 October 1958) arrived after a very tiring trip, the plane landing at a late hour in the night. I had arranged for our temporary stay for a week at one of the cottages at the Hawaiian Village Hotel in Waikiki. It was around midnight when we arrived there in the Fiat I had bought the week before. The cottages were surrounded by high hibiscus hedges, and were under a number of palm trees. Peggy was surprised the next morning when she heard cars that were driving down Kapiolani Boulevard just on the other side of our hedge. Living there for Peggy's first week in Hawaii was one of the few wise decisions I ever made, because Peggy and the children saw the good side of living in Hawaii right from the beginning. A week later, our furniture arrived and we moved into Navy quarters for junior officers at Pearl Harbor, but Peggy often took the children down to the Hawaiian Village for swimming and to visit some of the staff with whom she had become acquainted during our stay there.

During my tour at CincPac headquarters, where I, as aide to the second ranking officer, necessarily had access to the hundreds of high-level messages received from Washington and elsewhere across the world, I witnessed some of the seminal moments in our recent history. I have previously mentioned the Quemoy-Matsu incident which could well have precipitated a conflict with Communist China, but such was avoided by rapid, firm, and credible action at the highest levels, that convinced the leaders of China that the United States stood firmly by its commitment to the defense of Taiwan.

Although American involvement in Vietnam had begun early in President Eisenhower's first term, the focus at CincPac in 1959 was on Laos and Cambodia. The government of Laos was headed by General Phoumi Nosavan, who was playing both sides in order to gain the most benefits from the Communists and from the West, primarily the United States. Cambodia's government was directed by Prince Sihanouk whose erratic overtures to one side and then to the other caused much frustration at the headquarters.

Admiral Felt sent Vice Admiral Riley on a quasi-diplomatic mission to both countries in the summer of 1959. Riley was to assess the probability of either country falling under Communist influence, and while there, was to persuade each leader to sign a letter of commitment, guaranteeing their rejection of aid of any kind from the Communists.

Admiral Riley was accompanied by Stan Turner, while I remained at the headquarters to tend the daily routine of the office. Riley informed Admiral Felt by message that General Phoumi clearly was not intent on helping either side, his only interest appeared to be to gain as much for himself and his clique as possible and let Laos go whichever way the gods decreed. Riley then flew to Phnom Penh, Cambodia, for his meeting with Sihanouk.

The meeting with Sihanouk was inconclusive in its results, and Riley reported that Sihanouk had the delusion that he could outfox the Communists while accepting whatever they offered him. He assured Riley that there was no danger of Cambodia falling under the Communist mantle. Riley reported that he was unable to convince Sihanouk of the reality of his situation, nor was he able to get a signed commitment from either Laos or Cambodia.

I was periodically sending Admiral Riley reports of what was on the burners at headquarters, so he could keep abreast of things as they occurred. Nevertheless, Admiral Felt sent me to Wake Island to meet Admiral Riley on his return flight. I carried two brief cases of papers that Felt wanted Riley to get started on while on his leg from Wake to Hawaii.

I arrived at Wake the day before Riley's arrival, and took advantage of the time to get around the island and view the wreckage of guns and aircraft left from the war. The Marines on Wake, under the inspiring leadership of Colonel Devereaux, had put up a valiant defense, finally being overrun by the Japanese on 23 December 1941. In my trip around the small island, I realized that the island possessed no natural terrain for defense, adding to the heroic effort required by those fighting Marines. They had fought fiercely, knowing that they were on their own, there would be no relief force coming from Hawaii.

It was not until 1963 that the armed forces of the United States became actively involved in the struggle between the North and South Vietnamese governments in that divided country. The Communists of the North, headed by the venerable Ho Chi Minh, the man who had defeated the armed forces of France, now sought to unify all of Vietnam by both overt and covert conquest of the South. The armies of the North were well trained and well supplied by both the Soviet Union and China, while the military in the Republic of South Vietnam received minimal training and supplies from the United States. However, it was increasingly evident that, unless the South received additional arms and training, it would eventually be overcome by the superior strength of the North. Accordingly, President Kennedy established a full-fledged Military

Advisory and Assistance Group in Saigon, and sent several hundred Army trainers to begin the strengthening of the South.

Subsequently, Washington put many more American troops into Vietnam, but was not able to win the war, despite winning the battles. The American public lost its will to continue the war, and eventually our troops were withdrawn. Whether the war in Vietnam could have been won by the South remains moot, since the withdrawal of American forces, followed by the action of the American Congress to halt all aid to the South, ensured the defeat of South Vietnam and its subjugation by the North in 1975.

In January of 1960, I contracted spinal polio, causing paralysis of the muscles on my left side, ranging from my face to my foot. I was in Tripler Army Hospital for three months, followed by another two months of daily visits for rehab, leading eventually to my full return to duty after passing a physical test before a board of doctors at Tripler. I lost some muscle in my left foot, left leg, and in my back, but managed to compensate with other muscles, for the most part. During my sojourn in Tripler, our fifth child and first son, Mark, was born, with delivery made in Tripler by C-section.

The importance of the Pacific Command attracted a variety of high level officials as well as some well known figures in the entertainment and literary fields, including Bob Hope, John Wayne, and James Michener. From time to time I was detailed to escort one or another of the Washington officials, but I never had the opportunity to meet Hope or Wayne or Michener, no doubt due to my being junior to most of the other aides in the staff. Nevertheless, such visits were occasions for a lightening of the atmosphere for a few hours, amidst the many stressful occasions that were the norm. We also received a number of distinguished foreign officers and officials, and Vice Admiral Riley was usually tapped to be the official receptionist, with proper honors rendered. This required me to be at his side, so I met a number of these very interesting persons from a variety of countries. For the most part, they were very gracious and considerate, and made my chores easy.

Overall, duty at CincPac was for me a most valuable learning experience, providing insights to the workings of governments and the decision-making process within the Joint Chiefs of Staff in Washington and at the level of the Pacific Command, an experience that amply illustrated the tremendous responsibilities and difficulties of such an important command, and the courage and integrity needed by those at the top.

12

Back To Sea

We were enjoying life in Hawaii, and when it came time for me to return to sea duty, I was pleased to receive orders to USS Epperson (DD-719), home-ported in Pearl Harbor, part of Destroyer Squadron 25. I departed CincPac, and reported for duty on Epperson on 6 March 1961. After a short turnover period, I relieved Milt Schultz, class of 1950 and older brother of my classmate, Ernie Schultz, as Operations Officer and Senior Watch Officer.

Epperson was between WestPac deployments, and our underway time was spent completing the various drills and exercises required for workup for deployment readiness. In mid-August 1961, while Epperson was at sea off of Hawaii conducting gunnery exercises, I received message orders to USS Sproston (DD-577) as executive officer, to report by 22 August. Sproston was also in DesRon 25, and as Epperson was approaching its assigned berth in Pearl Harbor the following Friday afternoon, I was officer of the deck. I saw a flashing light message to Epperson from Sproston, which was already in port. The message was from signalmen to signalmen, and asked what kind of officer their new XO was. I called back to the signal bridge and told them to tell Sproston that LT Sagerholm is a real SOB. After Sproston rogered for that message, I then had the signal gang send an additional message, stating that LT Sagerholm also reads flashing light, and is the OOD. I watched through my binoculars as the signal gang on Sproston went scurrying below.

Sproston was commanded by Commander John Lyons, an officer with extensive experience at sea who was a most effective commanding officer. When I reported aboard, I was still in the rank of lieutenant, and CDR Lyons was obviously a bit skeptical of my ability to fill the XO billet, and with the ship just entering major overhaul at Pearl Harbor Naval Shipyard, the administrative load, for which the executive officer was responsible, would increase significantly due to large turnovers in personnel and the need to maintain correct and complete records of the work done while in the yard.

My previous experience in minesweepers as XO and CO now proved valuable as it enabled me to carry out my duties satisfactorily, and I thus gained the CO's confidence.

Major overhaul of a ship is never a pleasant experience, with the ship in disarray while work is being done that requires tearing down equipment. Welders require a crewman to attend them as a precaution against fire, a tiring, boring duty that quickly saps morale. Crew messing and berthing often are disrupted, and the need to berth and mess the crew off the ship tends to reduce crew cohesion and that special bond for one's ship that is a unique quality of being in the afloat Navy. Seagoing skills can also decline so it is necessary to allow for periods of seamanship training either on board another ship or in special training simulators. In short, extraordinary efforts in leadership must be exerted by the CO and the XO during this necessary part of a ship's life.

CDR Lyons was especially effective in keeping the crew in a high state of training and hjgh morale. I was very fortunate to be his XO during the first four months of my tour in Sproston., during which I learned a great deal from him, building on my previous experience.

In December, near the end of our overhaul period, CDR Lyons was relieved as CO by CDR John Tompkins, who came from shore duty in the Bureau of Naval Personnel. A very fine officer and a kind and courteous gentleman, he lacked the sea experience of his predecessor.

In early January, 1962, the ship was back together, the overhaul was completed, and it was time for us to go out to sea for trials of the various systems that had undergone repairs. The harbor of Pearl

Harbor can be likened to a doughnut, the hole of which is Ford Island. On the outer sides of the doughnut were the berthing areas allocated to submarines, destroyers, and larger vessels. At the south end of the doughnut is a straight channel that connects the harbor to the ocean, about a mile or so in length. The destroyer berthing was up a spur on the eastern side of the harbor, so destroyers had to take a right turn when coming into the harbor and then proceed to the Mike quay on the east side of the spur. It was common for DDs to be berthed in nests of three abreast, bow upstream or on a generally northeast heading. Berthing for ships in the Yard was just below the Mike quay, and this is where the Yard tugs had taken Sproston near the end of our overhaul, when our ship came out of dry dock.

Early on the day scheduled for our sea trials to begin, we set the Special Sea Detail, and I reported to the skipper that the ship was ready to get underway. Acknowledging the report, CDR Tompkins then asked me to take the conn. I ordered the mooring lines to be singled up, notified the engine room that we were about to get underway, then ordered the deck hands to take in lines one, three, and four. With line two still secured to the bollard on the quay, I commenced twisting ship by backing on the starboard engine and going ahead on the port. With the ship now at a sufficient angle to back away from the pier, I stopped all engines, ordered line two to be taken in, and with all lines now clear of the quay, we shifted colors from the forecastle to the foremast, and sounding one long blast on the ship's whistle, indicating we were underway, followed by three short blasts, to announce we were backing, I ordered all back one-third on the engines, and rudder amidships. With the ship now clear of the quay and the destroyers nested alongside it, I ordered the port engine stopped, then ahead one-third, rudder right full, and commenced twisting the ship to head for the channel. With the ship now pointing toward the channel, I ordered the starboard engine stopped, then ahead one-third and ordered the helm to steady on the course for the channel.

We increased speed to ten knots. Those sailors who were not engaged in operating the ship were lined up on deck in the uniform of the day, whites, and as we passed the Arizona Memorial that stands over the sunken battleship containing the remains of hundreds of her crew killed in the attack on Pearl Harbor, I ordered "Attention to starboard," then "Hand salute," rendering honors to those who had died for our country on that day when we were attacked by the Japanese fleet. Every Navy ship does so when passing the Arizona's remains.

When we passed the sea buoy, I ordered the sea detail to be secured, and the regular watch took over. The captain had been observing what we did, and seemed satisfied with what he saw.

We spent the next several days testing the various systems and equipment that had been overhauled, and then proceeded back into port. The captain again asked me to take the conn, so I brought the ship into the channel, and at the proper point, turned to starboard and headed for our assigned berth alongside the M quay. The wind was blowing steadily directly off the quay at about 15 to 20 knots, meaning that the ship would tend to be blown away from the quay. Under such conditions, the effect of the wind has to be countered by using the engines to drive the ship into its berth, so I continued the approach at 10 knots rather than slowing to 5, and as we neared our berth, I pointed the bow toward the quay, and ordered all engines to back full, at the same time ordering the deck hands to put over lines one and two. Lines were passed to the quay by throwing a small line, called a heaving line, attached to the mooring line, the heaving line having at its end a weighted "monkey fist" that was caught by the handlers on the quay, who then hauled in the line and secured it to the bollards on the quay. With those lines secured, I nudged the ship into the quay by touching the engines ahead and then stopping them. The bow was now in position so I twisted briefly on the engines to bring the stern in, and lines three and four were secured. The ship was now moored alongside and our colors were shifted to so indicate, the shift having occurred at the instant that the bow lines were made fast. The sea detail was secured from watch, and the in-port watch was set.

The captain had closely observed all this, and with the ship now moored, he asked me to accompany him to his cabin, where he then informed me that he was somewhat disturbed by the way I had moored the ship, saying he thought I had hot-dogged the landing, meaning I had used too much engine power, thus risking damage to the ship. I explained that the wind blowing off the quay made it necessary to use the engines to counter the effect of the wind. He seemed to have been unaware of the wind, and reiterated that while I had skillfully handled the ship, he did not like to see any hot-dogging, so I acknowledged and was dismissed.

The captain's reaction to the landing puzzled me, and I wondered if he thought we should have used tugs to push us in. I went back to his cabin, and asked him whether he would have preferred using tugs in windy conditions. He responded that the use of tugs had occurred to him, and then said that the APA on which he had last been to sea, in which he was the exec, had routinely used tugs to moor and to get underway. Now destroyer sailors take pride in being able to execute underways and moorings without use of tugs, that being considered landlubberly for a ship with the maneuverability of a destroyer. The expression on my face alerted him that his apparent preference for tugs was not something that would be popular with the crew, because he quickly said that he was not telling me to use tugs. He then changed the subject, and tugs were never again mentioned.

Once out of the yard overhaul, we spent the ensuing months getting the ship and crew ready for our next WestPac deployment, scheduled to begin in July, 1962.

We conducted anti-aircraft gunnery exercises, surface gunnery exercises, anti-submarine search and destroy exercises, engineering drills, damage control drills, fire drills, man overboard drills, and at times, worked with other ships in practicing formation tactics.

By May, the squadron commander found us ready for deployment, and the last week in June, the carrier Yorktown, accompanied by a division of four destroyers, arrived from San Diego. Our division of four destroyers spent the next four days exercising with them at sea, returning to port late on a Friday.

Saturday evening, the entire force took over the officers club for a farewell party that lasted well after midnight. Sunday was spent with our families, going to church and enjoying a leisurely dinner.

We boarded ship at 0600 Monday morning, the 2nd of July, 1962, and at 0800, immediately following morning colors, the force commenced getting underway. One by one, the destroyers departed from the Mike quay, with the Pacific Fleet band playing and the families waving and waving and waving until we were out of sight. It would be five months before we would see them again.

The force took up a circular screen formation with the Yorktown in the center, and then the carrier air wing commenced launching and recovering aircraft. We altered course to head into the wind, with speed increased to 28 knots. Normally, destroyers steamed with two of their four boilers on line, but when operating with a carrier, all four boilers were kept on line so that flight ops would not be delayed while the escorts brought all boilers on line. Of course, fuel consumption increased as a result, so every three days or so during the trip to Japan, the escorts came alongside the carrier to refuel from the carrier's fuel reserves.

The standard distance between ships for alongside refueling and replenishment was 80 feet, determined by the length of the fuel line, its length in turn determined by the weight that could be handled by the deck crews. The carrier maintained a speed of 15 knots, and it was the task of the destroyer to keep pace with the carrier, and also to keep the distance between the ships at or about 80 feet. The evolution began with the destroyer approaching the side of the carrier, and once alongside, a crewman on the carrier fired a shotgun especially adapted to shoot the heaving line over to the destroyer, where it was retrieved and hauled in by the DD's crewmen. The refueling hose was suspended from a heavy line, and it was this line that was attached to the heaving line. Once the refueling hose was secured to the refueling pipe that led to the fuel tanks, pumping commenced, and continued until the destroyer signaled for the pumping to stop. The destroyer was constantly increasing or decreasing speed by a few revolutions of the screws, or propellers to the landsman. The destroyer was also constantly adjusting heading by a degree or two left or right, in order to keep the proper distance from the carrier. It was demanding work, requiring constant attention by the conning officer, usually the captain or the officer of the deck (OOD). It was always a relief to see the refueling hose and the other lines being retrieved by the carrier, followed by the destroyer increasing speed and turning away to regain its assigned station in the circular screen.

Planes taking off and landing on the deck of a carrier is an inherently dangerous evolution, the degree of danger being determined by the sea conditions, the visibility, the velocity of the wind, the mechanical condition of the aircraft, and the pilot's skill. Night operations were especially difficult, with no horizon, low visibility, etc. One of the escorts was stationed a mile astern of the carrier when air operations were being conducted, its purpose being to rescue a downed pilot if a plane failed to land properly and went into the water. It was not uncommon for a pilot to be unable to escape from a sinking plane.

I never ceased to wonder at the Navy's ability to find that special breed of humanity that possessed both the skill and the daring needed in order to be a carrier pilot.

During our initial work-up with the carrier, night flight ops were being conducted, the night being without either moon or stars due to a heavy overcast. Helos were doing search tactics with sonobuoys they had dropped to try to detect a submarine we were exercising with. At about 2200, the exercise was secured, and I left my general quarters station in Combat Information Center, and went to my room that was on the main deck, starboard side aft. I was not there more than a minute when the captain called me to come to the bridge. When I went out on deck to go up to the bridge, I saw that all ships had turned on their topside lights and were sweeping the waters with searchlights. The captain told me that a helo had flown into the water, the pilot having apparently lost his awareness of the craft's altitude, there being no visible horizon, and probably had become too absorbed in the search for the submarine. We spotted four of the crew of six, clinging together in a circle. Our motor whaleboat was lowered and the downed aviators were retrieved. The two missing crewmen were never found.

The pilot was in bad shape, with severe shoulder and back injuries, so we carried him into the wardroom and laid him on the wardroom table. We notified the carrier of his condition, and at first light, a doctor and two corpsmen were brought over by a helo from the pilot's squadron. When we entered port, an ambulance was waiting and took him to Tripler Army Hospital, near Honolulu, where he eventually recuperated.

During our WestPac deployment, the ship visited a number of ports in Japan, including Yokosuka, Hakodate, Beppu, Osaka, and Sasebo. We also made visits to Hong Kong and to Subic Bay in the Philippines.

Sproston was in Sasebo, Japan, with its main engines torn down for heavy maintenance, when we received a message directing us to get all equipment and systems back to operational status, and when ready, to get underway and proceed at best speed to the Straits of Tsushima, there to set up an anti-submarine barrier patrol. This was a result of those tense days in October, 1962, known as the Cuban Missile Crisis. President Kennedy and Chairman Khrushchev of the Soviet Union were in a confrontation over the placing of Russian missiles in Cuba where they were within range of the entire eastern seaboard of the United States. The United States had instituted a naval blockade of Cuba to prevent any additional missiles from entering Cuba by ship. At the same time, the Pacific Fleet went to the highest condition of readiness, and set up choke points to intercept any Soviet submarines that might be transiting to the open Pacific waters, primarily from Vladivostok.

Japanese workmen swarmed over the ship, and in eight hours, we were ready for sea. We got underway and ran at flank speed, arriving at Tsushima a few hours before dawn. At flank speed, a ship cannot blow out the soot that accumulates in the stacks, and if enough collects there, the ship is treated to a display of fiery sparks blowing out of the stacks. And just as we began our patrol, the sky was lit up by our stacks spewing forth a steady stream of burning carbon sparks. The display lasted about ten minutes, when there were no more carbon flakes in the stacks. Fortunately, to the best of our knowledge, there were no ships in the vicinity.

After several days on the submarine barrier patrol with no contacts, the ship was electrified when the speakers came alive about 2100, "Now set Condition One, all hands man your battle stations. General Quarters! General Quarters! All hands man your battle stations!"

The ship was a scene of men rushing to their stations, hurriedly donning life jackets and helmets. I ran up one deck to Combat Information Center, where I was informed that sonar had picked up a submerged contact, as yet unidentified, but definitely a diesel submarine. The captain told me to call the contact on the underwater telephone, the UQC, and request the submarine to identify itself.

"This is USS Sproston, holding firm sonar contact on unknown submarine. Request identify yourself." There was no response on the UQC receiver.

I repeated the request, and again there was no response. A third attempt was met with the same results.

"Captain, this is CIC. Three requests have been made with no joy."

"Captain, aye. I will be down shortly."

A moment later, the captain entered, picked up the UQC telephone, and said, "Unidentified submarine, this is the CO of USS Sproston. Identify yourself immediately. Failure to do so will result in a full attack with depth charges."

After a few seconds, the UQC receiver crackled,: "USS Sproston, this is USS Queenfish. We will surface astern of you."

Shortly thereafter, the bridge reported seeing a submarine breaking the surface. Now on the TBS, our captain ordered Queenfish to come up on our port side. The submarine immediately increased speed, and as they came alongside some fifty yards away Commander Tompkins called to them on a loud hailer, "Queenfish, you came mighty damn close to being blasted!" After acknowledging, the submarine requested permission to proceed, and bearing off to our left, quickly submerged.

Queenfish was our only contact, and after ten days, we were ordered to return to Sasebo, and resume maintenance of the ship.

The Soviet Union, faced with the very real threat of a nuclear strike, had agreed to remove the offending missiles from Cuba. The world had come close to a major conflagration, and the Navy now returned to the daily routine of the Cold War.

In early December, the carrier and its eight destroyers formed up and headed east for home, with all hands looking forward to enjoying Christmas with their families. A great circle course is the shortest route to take on the globe that is the Earth, so the group navigator, with the admiral's concurrence, put the group on a course that curved well to the north before turning southeast to head for Hawaii. The higher latitudes are notorious for their stormy weather, especially in the winter. However, we seemed to be under the protection of Neptune as we steamed in relatively benign weather. As we reached the top of the circle, the group rendezvoused with an oiler to refuel for the run to Hawaii.

It may be better now, but in 1962, there was very little reporting of weather conditions in the area where we were, there being no weather satellites then to cover such areas. We were the last to go alongside the oiler, the time being about 1600. The day had started with a mix of clouds and sunshine, but now the sky was overcast and the wind began to increase. We were just completing our refueling when an extremely strong blast of wind hit the area, concurrent with blinding rain and sleet. The wind caused the oiler to veer away from us, in turn causing the refueling hose to break out of the pipe on Sproston, spraying heavy black fuel oil over the latter half of Sproston on the starboard side. LTJG Ray Belles, the head of the deck and gunnery department, was covered with oil from head to toe. As he stood on the deck of the bridge, reporting conditions to the captain, a pool of black oil was slowly collecting around his feet. The signalmen and quartermasters were responsible for the cleanliness of the bridge, and they were visibly upset about the trail of oil left by the unfortunate LTJG Belles.

We had executed an emergency breakaway, using axes kept at the ready for just such occasions to cut all lines connecting us with the oiler, and we now proceeded to our assigned station in the circular screen. The wind continued to increase, as did the seas. By midnight, we were taking heavy rolls while pitching up and down.

The scene at dawn was awesome, to say the least. The seas were now in excess of fifty feet from crest to trough. The ship would stagger up to the top of a wave, and then careen down the other side, to again stagger up the next wave. When at the top, all that could be seen of the other destroyers was a few masts appearing and disappearing, and the carrier was totally obscured by the driving, ice cold rain. The sea was dotted here and there with the orange life rafts that automatically inflated when hitting the water. All the destroyers lost some, swept overboard, and several lost all. I recalled the midshipman cruise in Missouri in 1951 when we passed north of Scotland on the way to Oslo, Norway. It was bad enough in the Missouri, but in a 2100 ton tin can, it was really bad. There being no interior fore and aft passage, one had to go on a weather deck. This meant that all who stood watches on the bridge or in CIC had to go up to the 01 deck, the main deck being constantly smashed by heavy waves. I climbed the vertical ladder from the torpedo room up to the 01 deck, and saw three young sailors clinging to the line rigged amidships. They were not moving, and when I approached them, they continued to hold fast where they were. I asked them where they were supposed to be, and was told they were reliefs for the bridge lookouts, but were unable to move for fear of being swept overboard. I took them forward, one by one, holding them with one hand and hanging on to the line with the other.

Later that day, I was sitting at my desk in my cabin, which was located on the main deck level, on the starboard side. A porthole was just above my desk in the starboard bulkhead, and was covered with a heavy brass porthole cover that was dogged fast with heavy brass clinchers. I had just risen from my chair when a huge wave came smashing down the starboard side, sweeping everything before it. It ripped the cover from the porthole and smashed the porthole, sending the heavy glass directly onto the chair from which I had just arisen. Gallons of water came crashing into my room and began spilling out into the after athwartship passageway, in which was located the large hatch leading down into the main engine control room. The hatch had a coaming about eight inches high, and I just managed to slam the hatch cover down before the water could flow into main control. If that had happened, the ship's electrical system might have been shorted by the water, and with the loss of electrical power, we would have been totally at the mercy of the storm And if I had been sitting in my chair, the porthole glass would have struck my head, with probable heavy injuries. The Repair Division placed a heavy wooden plate over the porthole, backed by a damage control four by four that was wedged against the steel stanchion nearby.

The group made an unscheduled stop at Midway for voyage

repairs, and then steamed on to Pearl Harbor. The families and Navy personnel waiting for us were shocked by the degree of damage we had sustained. But all was soon forgotten in the joy of our being home again.

13

Little Did We Know . . .

Commander Tompkins was relieved in May, 1963, and a few weeks later, I also was detached, having been relieved by my classmate, Chuck Horne. I had orders to the Junior Course at the Naval War College in Newport, Rhode Island, and looked forward to spending some time learning naval strategy and the writings of Mahan, Corbett, Clausewitz and Jomini. I knew that I could also obtain a master's degree in international relations while at Newport, something I had long looked forward to doing.

The small Fiat 600 we had been using would not be sufficient transportation for our family on the mainland, so before departing Hawaii, we arranged for the purchase of a Chevrolet Impala. The dealer in Honolulu advised against taking delivery in California due to the heavy tax there, and with our approval, arranged for delivery in Reno, Nevada, to coincide with our arrival from Hawaii.

With our Siamese cat, Desdemona, in a carrying cage, we boarded the bus in Oakland, California, for the trip to Reno. It was late evening when the bus pulled out. I was carrying Desdemona in her cage, concealed under my raincoat, since we had been advised when we bought the bus tickets that animals were not permitted on the bus. We had given her a tranquilizer provided by the veterinarian in Honolulu, but midway through the trip, late at night, she awoke and started meowing softly; we knew if we did not take her out of the cage, she would then live up to her name, Des the Moaner. The rear seat was vacant by now, so I quietly moved back there, and with most of the bus asleep, slipped her out of the cage. Our youngest daughter, Jeannine, had a kind of magic rapport with animals, so she sat with me and held Desdemona, who contentedly went back to sleep on Jeannine's lap. For the time being, all was well. Two hours later, in the wee hours just before dawn, we arrived in Reno. Jeannine was still holding Desdemona, and we placed her jacket over her arms as she walked forward and started to get off the bus. The driver smiled at her, and said he hoped our cat had enjoyed the ride. So much for our "deception."

We checked in at the motel where we had reservations, and they also kindly overlooked the cat, simply asking that we ensure that no damage occurred to our room. A big advantage to being in Reno with a family of six was the practice of the restaurants in the casinos to charge much lower prices than regular restaurants, so we ate all our meals in the casinos, and remarkably, gambled not one cent.

The car was two days late in arriving, so we had been in Reno four days and had just taken delivery of the Impala when Mark, our youngest who was just three and had never been on the mainland, developed a high fever. We took him to the clinic at the Fallon naval air station and were told that he had a strep infection which precluded any travel until it cleared up. We spent another five days in Reno, driving with the temporary Nevada tags on the car The Reno dealer suggested that, rather than getting regular Nevada tags, which were expensive to compensate for the lack of a sales tax, we drive up to Boise, Idaho, and there we could register the car and get tags for $35.

With Mark sufficiently well for us to travel, we headed out of Reno, much to the relief of the motel owner, who was very kind and patient during our extended stay, but who obviously was concerned about having any damage from the cat. Desdemona had been very good, and the room was left in excellent condition.

Leaving Boise, we headed east, in a new car with Idaho tags. This was to have an impact on events, because while we were en route, my orders were changed from the War College to duty as the naval aide to the Assistant Secretary of Defense for Manpower, an assignment that meant working in the Pentagon and living in the Washington area, a major change for us. Seems that the secretary, while riding overnight on a destroyer for the purpose of seeing how the Navy operated, had been told by his assistants that they had counted the number of watch stations, and they found that the ship had over three times that number of men aboard. Clearly, the Navy was way over-manned. With that information in hand, the secretary wrote a blistering letter to the secretary of the Navy, putting the Navy on notice to prepare to scale down its manpower numbers. The people in the Defense manpower office were embarrassed to learn that watches were stood on a one-in-three rotation, since no one could stand watch 24 hours a day, every day. The Defense manpower secretary thus accepted the Navy's offer of a naval aide who could advise him knowledgeably on matters naval. For whatever reason, the Bureau of Naval Personnel had chosen me to fill the billet.

BuPers was now faced with the problem of locating us and informing me of the change, so they called my parents in Baltimore, who told them that we intended to stay a few days with Peggy's widowed mother who also lived in Baltimore, but although they knew we were buying a new car, they did not know what model Chevrolet we had ordered. They also told the caller that we were picking up the car in Reno, so we probably had Nevada tags. My father suggested they call Peggy's mother, who might have better information as to where we were. I have always been a poor correspondent, and my parents had become accustomed to my failure to keep them informed of the details of my life, as it were.

Calls to Mrs. Herrlich elicited no better information, so they left word with her and with my parents to tell me to call the BuPers number they gave them as soon as possible.

It was a Saturday night, and we had been traveling for almost two weeks, taking our time to enjoy the sights, and were now checking in to the lodge at Wisconsin Dells, a resort area in upper Wisconsin. Since we would be arriving in Baltimore in a few days, I decided to call Mrs. Herrlich to alert her of the date we planned to arrive. She was in a state of near-panic, because the Bureau had been calling her daily, asking for any news of us. On the last call, received that morning, she was told that they were requesting the state highway police in Indiana, Ohio, and Pennsylvania, to be on the lookout for a Navy family bearing our description, driving in a new Chevrolet of unknown model, with Nevada tags. The impression left with her was that I was in serious trouble, which was why she was so concerned. She gave me the phone number, and emphasized that I had better call as soon as possible.

The officer who answered my call immediately began to berate me for not keeping them informed of my location, etc., so when he had finished his tirade, I asked him for his date of rank, he having identified himself as Lieutenant Commander K----. There was a few seconds pause, and then he gave me the date which showed him to be over a year junior to me, and when he understood that, he calmed a bit, and told me about my change of orders, mentioning that the change had occurred too late to change the shipping destination of our little Fiat and our household goods, which were scheduled to arrive in Boston in two weeks. He then told me that he had been instructed to tell me that I should arrive in BuPers on Monday, if possible, and not later than Wednesday. I told him that I would arrive Tuesday, given the distance to Baltimore and the fact I was traveling with the family. Before hanging up, I reminded him that I was on thirty days authorized leave, in a travel status, and had no obligation to keep BuPers informed of anything.

We arrived in Baltimore on Monday afternoon, and the next morning I checked in at the Bureau, expecting to then be sent over to the Pentagon. (BuPers was located in a set of buildings near Arlington Cemetery called the Navy Annex.) Instead, I was turned over to a commander and told to report to him daily for the next four to six weeks while receiving a series of briefings from every office in BuPers, to ensure I didn't cause any hiccups with Defense as to which office did what. Since there were plenty of officers of my vintage who had ample experience in the Bureau, I was puzzled as to why I, who had no experience there, had been selected, but no one seemed to have the answer, and I have never been able to find out the cause.

I was near the end of the series of briefings. It was a Monday morning. The phone rang, and I was greeted by Milt Schultz, the

Washington area detailer, who informed me that I was to be in the BuPers auditorium at 0745 Wednesday where I and six hundred or so other officers would be briefed by Vice Admiral Smedberg, Chief of Naval Personnel, prior to being interviewed by Vice Admiral Rickover for possible selection for nuclear power training. I told Milt that he had the wrong guy because I had not applied for nuclear power training. Milt assured me that he had made no mistake, and then told me the rest of the story.

The Navy, at the direction of President Kennedy, was building twelve ballistic missile submarines a year, with the goal of 41 to be completed by 1967. USS George Washington, originally intended to be an attack submarine, had been modified to carry sixteen vertical missile tubes, each missile to contain a nuclear warhead, which would give the United States a triad of nuclear missile launchers, namely, from missile silos buried deep in the ground, from B-52 bombers, and now also from submarines, the least vulnerable of the three due to the demonstrated ability to remain submerged and hidden for months at a time. Approximately two-thirds of the "41 For Freedom" were now in the fleet, and Rickover had exhausted the pool of acceptable officers from the diesel submarine community, and he refused to re-interview those whom he had already seen and had rejected. With the president's approval, Rickover now proceeded to set up interviews with members of the surface community, with the goal to be the selection of some 400 "volunteers."

And so it was on a bright Wednesday morning in the last week of August that six hundred or so naval officers, ranging in rank from ensign to lieutenant commander, assembled in the BuPers auditorium, where they were informed by Vice Admiral Smedberg, the Chief of Naval Personnel, why they were there. He stated clearly and emphatically that those selected for nuclear power training had no choice but to enter the program, and once in, it was hoped that they would volunteer for submarine duty. However, even if an officer did not volunteer for the silent service, he still had to undergo training in the nuclear power program.

There were about eight lieutenant commanders, as I recall, and we were told that we were to board the van that would take us to

Rickover's offices, located in a rundown temporary building behind the Navy Department building on Constitution Avenue.

We spent the next hour or so being interviewed by various members of Admiral Rickover's staff, a mix of civilians and officers. Then it was time for the interview by the "Kindly Old Gent" himself.

We were met by a group of captains and commanders who were in the Prospective Commanding Officer class, a three month course for officers going to their first command of a nuclear-powered vessel. I was taken in tow by Captain James L. Holloway III, who was going to command of the nuclear-powered carrier Enterprise. Captain Holloway carefully explained what I should and should not do in the interview, emphasizing that I should answer every question with a direct answer, and answer as completely and accurately as possible.

A female yeoman came out of the office, and said the Admiral was ready for my interview.

I opened the door, and as I walked across the room, I noted that my chair sat alone in the middle of the room, under a dangling light bulb, facing a battered wooden desk in the far corner, behind which sat Admiral Rickover. He motioned for me to sit down, and immediately began asking questions, such as "How old are you?" "Are you married?" "Do you have children?" After asking several questions about my class standing and my academic strengths and weaknesses, he asked me how long I had been married. "Sir, I have been married eleven years." He leaned forward, with a look of expecting more to come, and I recalled the advice to answer as completely as possible, so I added, "and two months." He leaned farther forward, and I was trying to count the days, when he burst out with "What the hell are you doing?"

" Sir, I am trying to count the days."

"You are what? What kind of a dumb answer are you trying to give me to a simple question? "

I explained that I was attempting to give him a complete answer, as I had been instructed to do.

He grabbed a book that was on his desk and threw it across the room, at which I inadvertently burst out laughing. Now he was really angry, or so it seemed. His face was red, and he yelled, "What are you laughing at?? Are you laughing at me??"

"No sir, " I replied, "it's just that this is so much like all the sea stories I have heard."

"So you think this is all just like sea stories, do you? Well, I'll tell you what you are going to do. You go out to the yeoman's office and you write me an official memorandum as to how long you have been married, to the hour! Now get out of here!"

Captain Holloway had been sitting in the corner across from the admiral, and he arose, took me by the arm, and helped me get the paper and pen I needed from the yeoman. He said his cubicle was just down the passageway if I needed him, and left.

I wrote the memo as directed, and looking at the clock to determine the hours, I noted that the time was 1045, the time that Peggy and I had exchanged our wedding vows, so I omitted the hours from my answer. I figured the admiral would think I was being a wise guy if I added zero hours. Furthermore, I assumed I had failed selection, so it was doubtful that Rickover would even bother to read my memo. I had not asked for nuclear power training, and I was not particularly bothered at not being selected.

I took the shuttle back to BuPers to debrief the submarine detailer, Captain "Sunshine" Aubrey. I told him of my exchange with Admiral Rickover and added I thought I had failed selection. The phone rang, and the yeoman who answered informed me that it was Admiral Rickover's admin assistant , asking for me.

I expected to be told that I had not been selected, so I was surprised when she said that the admiral wanted to know how many hours. I told her that it was zero hours, the memo having been written at the same time that I had been married. After a brief moment, she came back on the phone, and said,. "Admiral Rickover says that is an acceptable answer. Congratulations, you are in the program!"

I was a bit dumbfounded, but Aubrey had been listening in, and now grabbed the phone from me, congratulated me, and then asked if I was volunteering for submarines.

"Captain, I have astigmatism in my right eye, so I am not physically qualified for submarines." 20/20 vision was a strict requirement, or had been until then, because he then asked me how good was the vision in my left eye.

"My left eye is 20/20."

"Well, you know, periscopes only have one eye piece, so you're qualified."

Within a week, I had orders to Submarine School at the submarine base in Groton, Connecticut, to report on 16 September 1963, detaching from temporary duty in BuPers on 9 September.

We had enrolled the children in St. Bernadette School in Springfield, Virginia, where we had rented a house on a three year lease. We had bought curtains and some throw rugs, and were able to take only the rugs. The school was sympathetic and returned the tuition we had paid, but we lost our house deposit of five hundred dollars under the terms of the lease.

On the 9th of September, we set out for Groton and another adventure, courtesy of the US Navy.

14

The Silent Service

During the next two years, my patient wife and children moved from Springfield, Virginia to Groton, Connecticut; from Groton to Newark, Delaware; from Newark to Windsor, Connecticut; and from Windsor to Pearl Harbor, Hawaii. The children thus changed schools three times in less than two years, yet they handled the changes very well, a tribute to them and to their mother.

As senior officer in the 125th Officers Basic Submarine Class, I had the additional duty of mustering the class, and attending to similar administrative details.

One Monday morning, as I entered the class home room, the instructor informed me that Captain Woodall, the school commanding officer, wished to see me in his office.

"Good morning, sir."

"Good morning, Jim. We have a problem. The Sub Base CO has a daughter who has a horse that has been stabled in the CO's garage. As you know, his quarters are across the road from the O Club. The horse is missing, and there is reason to believe that some of your classmates may know where the horse is. I have been told by the CO that if the horse is not back in its stable by noon today, your entire class will be restricted until the horse is returned."

:Sir, request permission to muster the class at outside parade."

"Permission granted."

With the class in ranks in front of the school, I informed them of the situation, and asked for anyone who had knowledge of the horse's location to step out of ranks. Four young ensigns immediately did so.

Dismissing the rest of the class, I asked them to tell me what they knew.

"Well sir, we were at the club last night, and when we came out, we heard this poor horse whinnying and stomping around in that garage. I'm from Texas, sir, grew up on a ranch, and it seemed to me that the horse was not happy where it was, so we kind of liberated it."

"And where did you liberate it to?"

"Well sir, once we had the horse out, we did have trouble deciding where we should put her, it being a pretty cold night and all, so we finally decided she should be in some place warm."

"And where would that be?"

"Well sir, the best place we could think of, all things considered, was the BOQ boiler room. That's where she is, sir."

After looking at them for a half minute or so, I asked them if they were aware of what else was in the boiler room by now. The lad from Texas nodded and said he volunteered to clean it up. So we all went to the boiler room, where the missing mare was sleeping in a corner.

I detailed two others of the group to do the cleaning, and took the Texan and his buddy with me and the horse, back to the Sub Base CO's quarters. Traffic stopped as we marched the horse down the middle of the road.

After they had led the horse back into its stall in the garage, they started to walk back to the school.

"Whoa, gents, you have an apology to make."

For the first time, they looked a bit concerned, but reluctantly walked up onto the porch, and when Mrs. CO opened the door, they told her they were sorry and that the mare was back in its stable. Mrs. CO was very gracious, and thanked them for returning her daughter's horse. She asked us if we would like a cup of coffee, but I explained that they now had to go to the CO and apologize to him.

"Oh no, don't do that! I will tell him about it when he comes home for lunch. Thank you again."

A visibly relieved pair of ensigns walked back to the school, their demeanor one of humility and gratitude.

The training at Submarine School was geared to the experience level of a junior officer, so much of it was not needed by the lieutenant commander group. We thus had an abbreviated course, focused solely on the basics of submarining. After several weeks of drills on the diving trainer, we went to sea on the school boat, a WWII diesel boat commanded by a 1950 graduate of the Naval Academy. When we arrived on board that Monday morning, the crew was naturally curious as to why a group like us were being trained on their boat, so our every move was given a good deal of scrutiny by all hands.

It took several hours to reach water deep enough in which to submerge, so we spent the time keeping the navigation plot in the conning tower, just below the bridge. When we reached the diving point, we were told to come up to the bridge, where the captain rehearsed with us the procedure to be followed when diving the boat. We were to take turns as the surface OOD on the bridge, and when the order to dive came, we were to acknowledge the order, and sound the diving alarm. Then we were to check as each man from the bridge watch descended to the conning tower, this to be done quickly, and when all had gone below, we were to follow, shutting and securing the bridge hatch cover, and announcing, "Last man down, hatch secured, sir!"

The weather was cold and rainy, not very pleasant, and we were dripping wet on the bridge. I was the first to make the dive, so I remained on the bridge while the rest of our group went below. I relieved the OOD and reported having the deck to the captain in the conning tower below. Shortly thereafter, the order to dive came. I acknowledged the order, and sounded the diving alarm. Almost immediately, I heard the ballast tank vents opening and the boat began to submerge, rather rapidly it seemed to me. It also seemed that the lookouts were not moving very quickly, but were taking their time getting down the hatch into the conning tower. In the meantime the sea was rapidly closing over the boat, and I was getting a bit concerned about being able to get below and shut the hatch before the bridge and the hatch were under water. The diving trainer had not prepared us for this aspect of diving. As the head of the second lookout disappeared down the hatch, I literally jumped into the hatch feet first, grabbed the lanyard attached to the under side of the hatch cover, and fell feet first the rest of the way down, foregoing the use of the ladder. As I did so, I pulled on the lanyard and slammed the hatch cover shut, reached up, dogged it tight, and announced, "Last man down, hatch secured, sir!" Without realizing it, being dripping wet, I was also spraying water on all those nearby, including the captain. With a grin, he said, "Well, you made quite a splash on your first dive."

Submarine School was followed by Nuclear Power School at Bainbridge, Maryland. So, for the third time in my Navy life, I found myself back at the site where I began the wearing of Navy blue. We rented a house in nearby Newark, Delaware, and entered the children in the public schools there. It being early May when we arrived, they spent only a few weeks in the classroom before school ended for the summer.

I commenced school on 12 May 1964 in a classroom located in an old World War II barracks, not far from the barracks where I had lived while in boot training in 1946. The dusty drill field had been paved with macadam, and was now a parking lot.

Nuclear Power School was intended to give nuclear power operators a good grounding in the theory of the nuclear power process. The school, in my opinion, was much too layered in theory, expressed in esoteric mathematical equations, and for me at least, was not a good use of time.

The basic process is not complicated and is readily understood when described in terms of the power cycle that occurs in a pressurized water nuclear reactor. The reactor core contains radioactive fuel that emits radiation. The core is immersed in water that is pressurized by centrifugal pumps. The radiation emitted by the radioactive fuel is absorbed by the pressurized water, causing the water to become heated well above 212 degrees Fahrenheit, the temperature at which water becomes steam at atmospheric pressure. The water, called the primary coolant, and which is pressurized by the continuous closed flow impelled by the primary coolant pumps, thus becomes superheated without flashing to steam. The primary coolant flows from the reactor to the heat exchanger where it flows through a set of tubes in the heat exchanger that are surrounded by the water of the secondary coolant. This water, being at atmospheric pressure, flashes to steam which then is used to drive the main turbines. The energy drop across the turbines cools the secondary coolant sufficiently to return it to the liquid state, where it is again cycled through the heat exchanger and the process repeats. The amount of heat, or energy, transferred from the reactor to the primary coolant is controlled by moving the control rods in or out of the reactor, the farther they are moved out, the greater the transfer of energy, the function of the rods being to absorb the radiation from the reactor to a greater or lesser degree, depending on how far the rods are withdrawn. The process is shut down by fully inserting the rods into the reactor.

Our instructor was a young lieutenant who held a doctorate in nuclear physics. His method of teaching was to rapidly write an endless equation across the blackboard with his right hand while erasing what he had written with his left hand. As he wrote and erased, he delivered a monologue designed to explain the equation, which in turn was intended to explain the process of nuclear decay or radiation and how it was applied in the nuclear power process. I quickly learned that I simply could not keep up with him and still note what he was saying, so I dropped the effort to copy the equation and just wrote notes that recorded his monologue, more or less. To get a grade above 3.0 on a scale of 4.0, it was necessary to reproduce the equations he scribbled as well as describe the process in English. Since I only gave the answers in long-hand English on the tests, the highest grades I attained were 3.0, and I finished the 24 weeks of classes with a final grade of 3.0 and a standing of 52 in a class of 70. This was the worst I ever did in any naval class, and I was not exactly thrilled with being in the nuclear power game.

While I was enduring the drudgery of classes, Peggy was making the best of life in Newark, which is not far from Delaware Park and its periodic sessions of horse racing. I should point out here that Peggy had grown up in a household where her very genteel grandmother and mother were avid fans of horse racing, to the extent that they had their own bookie. So when the ponies were running at Delaware Park, Peggy and her mother and two sisters, who drove up from Baltimore, went to the track and engaged in betting, using their own tried and true system of picking winners, consisting of how much they liked the colors of a particular horse, the way the horse carried itself while going to the start, the way the jockey looked, and other similarly scientific criteria understood only by them.

One afternoon, they were enjoying the day at the track, where they had won in three of the first four races. Two men sitting in the row below them were using various scratch sheets and other sources of information designed to be used in making an informed decision on picking winners, but they were so far winless. As the horses were making their parade to the starting gate, one of the men turned and said, "Okay, ladies, who do you like in the fifth race?" He took their recommendation and was crowing delightedly when he won while his friend, who had stuck with the sheets, lost again. They picked two more winners, making a total of six winners out of the seven races that day. The two men never did figure out the Herrlich system, despite the efforts of the ladies to explain it. That was probably the most successful betting that the Herrlich ladies did, but overall, they never were net losers. In fairness to those two gents, I confess that I never understood the Herrlich system either, which I think involved more intuition than anything else.

September found us on the move again, this time back to Connecticut, where I was assigned to the S1C reactor in Windsor Falls. There I would spend the next 26 weeks learning every facet of the plant and its operation as prescribed in the Reactor Plant Manuals, culminating in the dreaded oral examination before a board of four officers. The oral tested the student's knowledge of both the proper operation of the plant and the correct procedures to follow in the event of a casualty to the plant. Successful completion of the oral resulted in qualification as Engineering Officer of the Watch, the engine room equivalent of the Officer of the Deck on the bridge of a ship or in the control room of a submarine.

I did a bit better here than at Bainbridge, finishing with a grade of 3.42 and a standing of 8 in a class of 36.

We rented a Cape Cod style house in Windsor, and watched the snow pile up as the winter wore on. By the time spring arrived, the snow had reached over five feet where it had not been removed, and snow was the routine rather than the exception. The children enjoyed ice skating outdoors and were also once again in new schools. Lisa and Jeannine were in parochial school, but Denise had to attend public school because there was no room for her in her grade at the church school. Connecticut public schools have an excellent reputation, so I was a bit shocked when Denise came home with a note from her teacher that requested some stamps and coins be sent to her from my new duty station, which was Pearl Harbor, Hawaii.

We spent a few days with our families in Baltimore, and then set out by auto for Oakland, California, a trip that took about ten days. At Oakland, we boarded a Navy transport ship for the voyage to Hawaii, a voyage of six days during which we could relax and enjoy being at sea. When we arrived in Honolulu, the wardroom of USS Seadragon (SSN-584) and the wives were waiting to greet us with leis and warm alohas, typical of a ship with an outstanding skipper in Commander Ray Engle, and an equally outstanding executive officer, Lieutenant Commander John Will. Claire Engle and Linda Will immediately took care of Peggy, making her feel among warm friends, and helping with the details of getting settled in temporary quarters in Honolulu. Once again, I was very fortunate to be assigned to a ship, a submarine in this case, with great officers and crewmen.

This time, we bought a house rather than renting or going into Navy quarters. The development known as Foster Village consists of private homes built in the early 1960s. Located just a few miles from Pearl Harbor, it was a popular location for homes bought by naval officers. 1376 Uila Street was sold to us by its owner, an Army colonel, for $19,500, two thousand above its original cost. It was one story, with three bedrooms and a covered carport which had been converted to a closed fourth bedroom. Two baths, a kitchen, dining room and living room completed the interior, and the exterior was enclosed on the sides and rear by a high hedge of flowering hibiscus. The house was L-shaped, with the L enclosing a large paved patio in the rear. The front was open, with a small pond and waterfall flowing over lava rocks, a small electric pump providing the flow. Brightly colored carp swam in the small pool. An enclosed lanai (porch) looked out over the pond and waterfall, the pleasant tinkling of the water providing a nice complement to the cool breeze that came off the mountains a few miles to the north of us. A plumeria tree and a Norfolk pine set off the front. This was our home for the next five years or so.

The principal focus of my time on Seadragon was qualification, both in learning the systems of the boat and in learning the art of the submariner. I was senior in rank to everyone on board except the skipper; even the XO was two years junior to me. This could have posed an awkward situation, but the officers and the crew understood why I was there and there were no problems, except for one minor incident.

I initially was assigned to the Engineering Department as the Main Propulsion Assistant, the officer who is the division officer for the machinist's mates who operate the engineering plant. My goal while assigned there was to learn the plant and to qualify as Engineering Officer of the Watch. Because of my unique status, all on board kept tabs on my progress, so it was no surprise when I sat down at the wardroom table one day for lunch and I was asked by one of the officers how I was doing. I told him I was doing okay, and had received a check-off that morning on the atmosphere control system.

One of the officers at the table was a LTJG who was in the Operations Department. I heard him say, "Hey, NQP, pass the salt." Then I heard him repeat it, adding, "I'm talking to our surface puke, but he seems to be deaf." NQP is a derisive term for a non-qualified person, with the "P" standing for "puke."

I looked at him, and then stood up from the table. "Come out into the passageway with me."

He looked down the table for support, but seeing none, he stood up and followed me out of the wardroom. I ordered him to stand at attention, and then forcefully explained to him that, regardless of my qualification status, I was still a lieutenant commander, two grades senior to him, and that I awaited his apology. To his credit, he acknowledged his error, and forthrightly apologized. We returned to the wardroom, and there were no more incidents like that.

After three months aboard, I qualified as EOOW, and was then transferred to the Operations Department, where I relieved the departing Ops Officer The crew, who of course knew of the confrontation between the LTJG and me, watched to see how I treated the young officer. I learned later that there was some disappointment when they saw me treating him as if nothing had happened between us, but they also respected me for not using my position to hammer him.

Shortly after I moved into the Operations billet, we departed for a special operations assignment in the western Pacific, during which I learned a great deal about the art of operating a submarine. It was an exciting and fascinating experience, and I am sorry that I can say no more about it.

We returned to Pearl Harbor shortly before Christmas, and learned that we were going to be sent to the naval shipyard at Bremerton, Washington, for major overhaul of our main engines, to depart Pearl just after Christmas. This meant that we would again be separated from our families for several months, after having been away for four months.

The wives took it in stride, however, and each family, at their own expense, flew to Bremerton, my own family included. Peggy had rented our home to a trio of female school teachers, and called me to say that she and the children would be arriving at SeaTac Airport on a Sunday evening. I borrowed a car from one of the officers who had a friend in Bremerton who had loaned him her car. When I arrived at SeaTac, I learned that fog was expected within the hour, at about the time that Peggy's flight was due to arrive.

The forecast proved to be accurate, and the flight was diverted to a field in Oregon to await the expected clearing of the fog at SeaTac within the hour. SeaTac was blanketed in a thick fog for about 30 minutes, and then the fog began to thin and disappear. We were told that the flight was on its way to Seattle, and that the fog was expected to return shortly after the expected time of arrival of the flight, meaning that the window of visibility would be open only for a short while.

In the event, it was a white knuckle experience. Just as the aircraft was approaching SeaTac, the fog rolled in, again blanketing the field. The pilot decided to come in anyway, and we could hear the plane as it descended but we could not see it until just before it landed on the runway. Cheers erupted, and we all finally greeted our anxiously awaited arrivals.

Now, I was faced with the decision either to drive back to Bremerton in the fog, or await its clearing, the time of which was uncertain. The children and Peggy were clearly very tired, so I put them in the car, and for the first mile or so, I hung out the window, keeping the car on the road by watching the side of the road as I drove. I had rented a two-bedroom furnished apartment in Bremerton, in which the landlord had installed two bunk-beds for the children, and when we finally arrived there, all were fast asleep. It took only a few minutes to get them into bed, and the feeling of having them all with me was very, very comforting.

The three months in Bremerton was like an extended vacation, in the sense that we were enjoying a different place under different living arrangements. We walked or took buses to wherever we went, and although the children were in another strange school, they made friends easily and seemed to thrive in the experience. Surely I was blessed with a wonderful Navy wife, and children who always positively responded to our guidance.

After our return to Hawaii, our neighbors gently informed us that they had dubbed the trio who had rented our place, "The Wild Bunch." Seems they had a party every weekend, and rode motorcycles up and down Uila Street, among other activities. However, they did no damage to our home.

On a typically bright June day in 1966 in Pearl Harbor, the officers and crew of Seadragon stood in formation along the quay at the Submarine Base, while I received the gold dolphins of a submarine officer, and at the same time, I was promoted to commander. After Peggy and the skipper had attached the dolphins and changed the shoulder boards on my dress whites, the crew picked me up and "baptized" me in the not-too-clean waters of Pearl Harbor. I climbed back on to the quay, and seeing Peggy laughing at the sight I made, to the delight of the crew, I wrapped my dripping arms around her, getting her new muumuu thoroughly wet with the aromatic waters of the harbor.

New orders followed for duty as executive officer of the Mariano G. Vallejo (SSBN-658)(Blue), under construction at Mare Island Naval Shipyard, Vallejo, California. I was detached from Seadragon in mid-July, 1966.

After ten intensive weeks of instruction on the Fleet Ballistic Missile Weapons and Navigation System at Dam Neck, Virginia, I arrived at Mare Island, where the boat was due to be commissioned in December. The commanding officer was Commander Doug Guthe, class of 1949, and a good friend of my brother, also class of 1949. Doug Guthe was the sharpest CO I ever served under, with a keen intellect and a memory for facts and figures that was truly exceptional. We quickly established an excellent working relationship that made the many tasks of an XO easier to perform.

Mare Island was one of the Navy's top shipyards, and the final steps of construction progressed smoothly.

In late November, a large covered barge was moored alongside our submarine. At the same time, a civilian from Vice Admiral Rickover's staff came on board and informed me that he had authorized the rental of six teletype-writers, the kind which were fed a tape that actuated the machine and automatically printed what was on the tape. He had six tapes, one for each machine, with each tape containing the same text of a three page letter, prepared by Rickover's staff, a letter that described the sea trials of a newly built submarine, and was to be sent to some 400 important personages, ranging from the Queen of England to various senators and Congressmen. I was informed that the preparation of those letters for the admiral's signature while we were on sea trials would be my primary duty. I was to ensure that each letter contained no errors and that the margins of each page aligned perfectly with one another when held up before a light. I was also told to have our supply officer obtain five pounds of white seedless grapes, two pounds of hard lemon drops, and material for shipping six sets of wash khakis. The latter were to be shipped to exceptionally important persons after being worn by Admiral Rickover during the sea trials.

I informed the CO of these requirements, and was told to drop everything else in order to ensure that there were no glitches with the letters and the other requirements. I borrowed some yeomen and electronics techs from the other boats in the yard, and by the time that the admiral arrived, which was the night before trials were to commence, we had all the letters completed, the grapes and lemon drops were on board, and the boxes for shipping the khakis were in the hands of LT Russ Duvall, our very competent supply officer. I moved out of the XO cabin and the admiral moved in.

The next six days at sea were a blur for me of reading each letter to ensure no typos existed, and then holding the three sheets in front of a bright light to further ensure the perfect alignment of each page. I took batches of ten letters at a time in to the admiral for his signature, collecting those that were signed, and checking that the letter addressed to person X was placed in the proper envelope for person X. Russ collected the khakis from the admiral and we checked to see that they also were placed in the right box for shipping, each accompanied by a short hand written note from the admiral.

From time to time, Rickover would go aft to see how the trials were doing, giving me and the yeoman a break for a while. All went well, and we returned to port at the shipyard, where Admiral Rickover commended the skipper with his usual curt words, but nevertheless it was good to get a commendation from him, however short.

Both the Blue and the Gold crews now turned to the task of readying for the commissioning, set for 16 December. Commander Jack Nunneley, class of 1951, and his XO, Lieutenant Commander Mort Botshon, worked side by side with Doug Guthe and me, handling the myriad details involved in a commissioning, not the least of which for us was how to take care of the various offers from the Napa Valley wineries to provide champagne and other wines for the banquet, being careful to treat each equally. We soon saw that the only way to achieve equal treatment was to allow each winery to give us whatever they wished, resulting in a stock of various brands of champagne that far surpassed the needs of the banquet. Various ship parties and social functions were well supplied with champagne for several months afterward.

The commissioning and the banquet proceeded smoothly, and were well attended by the regional politicians and other local luminaries, as well as the several flag officers in the area. The ship's sponsor, Miss Patricia McGettigan, a direct descendant of General Vallejo, delivered a gracious speech and presented the ship a silver set that had belonged to her distinguished ancestor.

With that behind us, we now began the task of readying our submarine for its mission. This included a trip through the Panama Canal to test the missile system at the facility located at Cape Canaveral, a transit done by the Blue crew, who then carried out the first test of the missile system by successfully launching a missile.

While at Cape Canaveral, we received the sad news that the Gold crew Missile Officer had been lost off the coast of northern California when the boat he and some friends were fishing from was capsized by a storm.

The Gold crew flew to Florida where they relieved the Blue crew, and prepared to do their missile launch, after which they would bring the boat back to Mare Island via the Panama Canal.

We in the Blue crew returned to Vallejo in the same chartered aircraft that had brought the Gold crew, and used the time to make the arrangements for relocating to Pearl Harbor, our assigned homeport. The families who had been living on the shipyard, including mine, had already gone to Hawaii, and Peggy and the children were back in our home in Foster Village.

The mission of the fleet ballistic missile submarine is totally different from that of the attack submarine. The latter is engaged in the day-to-day fleet operations, as well as special operations involving a variety of covert tasks. The SSBN, on the other hand, has the primary mission of providing a credible retaliatory nuclear response in the event that the United States comes under a nuclear attack or the threat of such, thus assuring that any potential hostile nation that possesses nuclear weapons can see that it cannot attack us without suffering a nuclear response. The nuclear force of the United States is comprised of inter-continental ballistic missiles located in fixed silos deep in hardened structures buried in the ground, the nuclear bomber force, and the fleet ballistic missile submarine force. This nuclear triad, by its diversity, gives increased survivability to the force as a whole, with the submarine element being the most survivable of the trio. It was the assured response of a nuclear strike that deterred the onset of major conflicts during the period known as the Cold War, the period during which the United States and its NATO allies contested the attempts of the Communist Soviet Union and its proxies to spread communism across the world.

In order to keep the SSBN at sea and ready to launch for a maximum period of time, each SSBN has two crews assigned, Blue and Gold, and is based at a location that permits rapid assumption of ready status once at sea. Thus, the SSBNs in the Pacific were forward based at Guam, although their homeport was Pearl Harbor. The families of SSBN crews lived in Hawaii, and the crews flew back and forth between Guam and Hawaii. Each on-crew period, the time when a crew was operating the boat, was approximately three months in duration. This period of time included a five day turnover of the boat to the oncoming crew, a ten day prep period, and sixty or more days on patrol.

I made two patrols in Vallejo, patrols which gave me valuable experience prior to going to command of an SSBN.

As the second patrol neared its end, we received orders to proceed south to the Pacific test range where we would launch a test missile that had a test warhead in place of a nuclear warhead. We had to cross the Equator, so we improvised a Crossing the Line Ceremony for the induction of the pollywogs on board into the realm of King Neptune. The CO, the Chief of the Boat, Senior Chief Quartermaster John Harned, and I were all shellbacks, as were most of the other chief petty officers and senior petty officers. However, we were outnumbered by the pollywogs by at least a 2-to-1 ratio, and as we approached the Equator, the pollywogs staged a well-planned and well-executed revolt, led by the few chiefs who were not shellbacks. Using canvas webbing kept on board for loading stores, they set up an enclosure in the missile compartment by wrapping the webbing around several of the large vertical tubes, making a space large enough to hold four prisoners.

I was rousted out of my bunk around 0200 on the day of the crossing, and was escorted to the "prison" by four masked crewmen. Masked or not, it was easy to identify them by their voices and general appearance. I joined the captain in our "cell," where I was offered a cup of coffee by our captors. After an hour or so, the rebels appeared with a paper that would grant them amnesty from any reprisals, in return for which they would release us. The captain signed it, and then handed it to me for my signature. Instead of signing my name, I scribbled James A. Seaman and handed it to the rebels, who took it without checking it, and they released us.

A mainstay of the ceremony is having the pollywogs run the gauntlet, after which they crawl through a mess of garbage called the "slop chute," and then they must kiss the belly of the Royal Baby, who is usually a big hairy individual with some foul smelling ointment smeared on his belly. They are then ready to be presented to King Neptune and his consort, and after making the proper obeisance to the Royal Worthy Ruler of the Vast Realm of the World's Waters, they are admitted to the privileged ranks of the shellbacks.

I took station at the end of the slop chute, and when the first of the four who had captured me appeared, I took his arm and handed him over to the King's Sheriff, declaring that he did not seem to be ready yet to approach the Royal Family. He protested and produced a copy of the amnesty sheet, claiming that he should not be subject to reprisals. I asked the Sheriff to examine the signatures on the amnesty sheet and read aloud the names on the signatures. When he read "James A. Seaman," the erstwhile captor grabbed the sheet, and for the first time, looked at the signatures. He was the picture of despair, so I suggested that he only be required to run the gauntlet again, omitting a repeat crawl through the slop chute. When he reached the end of his session with the Royal Family, I was standing nearby, and he asked me how I had known that he was one of the captors. I told him that as XO I knew all and saw all. I think he only partially disbelieved me.

Following the second patrol of the Vallejo Blue Crew, I received orders to command of Kamehameha (SSBN-642)(Gold), via a three month course of instruction for prospective commanding officers going to their first command of a nuclear-powered vessel, the course being under the personal supervision of Admiral Rickover at his headquarters in Washington, DC.

In a very emotional ceremony, for me at least, the crew presented me a Rolex wrist watch, engraved on the back with my initials, rank, billet, ship's name and hull number, and the date, "3-68." I have worn the watch ever since, a cherished keepsake.

The day I arrived in Washington to report to Rickover's headquarters was the day of the riots in Washington, resulting from the assassination of Martin Luther King. I was in my dress khaki uniform, walking down Constitution Avenue, the only person there so far as I could see. A pall of heavy black smoke hung over the city, and as I proceeded on foot toward the Navy headquarters building, I saw an Army tank come grinding around the corner ahead. The tank was buttoned up, and as it approached me, the top hatch opened and a figure rose up out of the tank, gesturing for me to stop, which I did. A lieutenant climbed down and asked me if I was on official business. I explained that I had orders to report to Admiral Rickover's headquarters on this date, and showed him a copy of my orders. He saluted, said I could go on, and added that I should be careful if I saw anyone in the streets. As the tank clanked away, I felt as if I were on a movie set, the whole scene was so unreal

I checked in, and was told that a furnished apartment on Virginia Avenue was available for me, so with the address in hand, I proceeded up Virginia Avenue, where I found the landlord anxiously awaiting me. I signed the three month lease, gave him the required deposit check, and settled in for the riot to dissipate. The rioters did not bother the residential areas, evidently being interested only in the business section where loot was available. We were told to remain indoors the next day, and by the following day, all that remained of the riot were the burned out stores and their smashed windows.

The city returned to normal activity during the day, but a ten o'clock curfew made the evenings artificially quiet, with only cars and taxis carrying last minute diners to their abodes. Some of the restaurants were without sufficient electricity to turn on lights, having only enough power from emergency generators to operate stoves and refrigerators. It was rather nice to have dinner in a restaurant lit only by candle light, especially since one effect was to create an atmosphere of intimacy, causing conversations to be spoken much more softly than usual.

Two other incidents occurred during my days in "charm school."

Following the death of Reverend King, his followers, under the guidance of several of his minister colleagues, organized a march from Selma, Alabama, to Washington, where they then camped within the mall that extends from the Washington monument to the Lincoln Memorial, from which they sortied daily to give improvised parades and rallies along Constitution Avenue and on Pennsylvania Avenue near the White House. They traveled in colorfully decorated farm wagons drawn by horses, adding a quaint touch to their demonstrations. There was no violence, and the city seemed to take their presence in stride.

The other incident was the tragic loss of USS Scorpion, a nuclear attack submarine that had been deployed to the Mediterranean. On the day of its scheduled return, the families of the officers and crew gathered on the pier at Norfolk, awaiting their loved ones whom they had not seen for months. The time for their arrival came and passed, with no boat in sight. Then came the ominous message from Commander Submarine Force, Atlantic, that a search and rescue mission had been initiated. By nightfall, it was becoming clear that Scorpion was not returning, ever. All messages to her were met with silence.

The cause of Scorpion's loss remains unresolved, although the stricken hull was located in very deep water near the Azores, near her homeward track, and a committee of experts conducted an exhaustive investigation. Thresher had been lost during a test depth dive in 1963, and now came the Scorpion tragedy in 1968. Were our submarines the victims of poor construction, poor design, inadequate training, etc., etc.?

These and other questions were pursued in Rickover's headquarters, and several improvements to our submarines resulted, but it did not appear that, absent these improvements, Scorpion's design contained any fatal flaws. In the event, no submarines of the U.S. Navy have been lost since then, and the U.S. submarine force continues to be a top fighting force true to the legacy of our Second World War forebears.

Having completed the course for prospective commanding officers, I, together with my family, once again set a westward course across our great country, this time taking the southern route through the southeast and southwest, covering about 400 miles per day. We were approaching Bakersfield, California, when the transmission of our Chevrolet Impala decided it had had enough, and we ground to a stop. Within fifteen minutes, a highway patrolman came by, stopped, and called for a tow truck. An hour later, we checked in at a motel in Bakersfield, after being told by the mechanic who checked our car that it would take at least five days to fix the transmission.

Bakersfield is not exactly a tourist's paradise, sitting on the edge of the desert with one and two story buildings of monotonous form, colorless and lacking in grace as to appearance. This was 1968, and the town today may well be much improved, but that was its appearance then as we settled in at the motel. Swimming at the motel's pool was a daily event for the children, and was probably the only thing that kept them from being a restless, unhappy group. I spent the time reading some novels I picked up at the local drugstore, and Peggy contented herself with joining the children at the pool.

The car was finally ready to go, and early the next morning, we were on the highway, heading for Oakland where we were scheduled to board an aircraft for our third return to Hawaii. We had notified our tenants that we were returning so the house was waiting for us when we arrived. After the extended absence, it was good to again be back in our home.

The Kam Gold crew was in the off-crew status, occupying the assigned offices located on Ford Island. The day after our return, I checked in and Captain Bob Dickieson and I began the process of turning over command. The date for the change of command was set for two weeks in the future, to be held in the outdoor area among the barracks on the submarine base at Pearl Harbor.

A change of command is a formal ceremony where the officer being relieved reads his orders detaching him from command and sending him to his next duty, accompanied by suitable remarks in which he traditionally praises his crew and welcomes the incoming commanding officer. The latter then reads his orders, turns to the out-going CO, salutes, and says the time-honored words, "I relieve you, sir!' The salute is returned with the words, "I stand relieved." The new CO delivers his remarks, usually including commendatory comments about the departing CO, and the intent of the new CO to do his best for the ship and the crew.

Following the ceremony, Bob and I with our wives welcomed

the guests in a reception line. There were several rear admirals in attendance, and the first of them congratulated Bob and then me, and turning to Peggy, who was at my right, he extended his hand and said the well-worn phrase, "Nice to see you again." Peggy, in her inimitable way, looked at him and replied, "I don't think we have ever met." To the admiral's credit, after a split-second of being off-balance, he quickly recovered and said, "In that case, may I say it is a pleasure to meet you." With a smile and a shake of the hand, he moved on, and I inwardly heaved a sigh of relief. His graceful handling of what could have been an awkward situation, impressed me, and provided me a valuable lesson.

Three weeks later, the long-awaited day arrived when the Gold crew boarded the PanAm charter flight for Guam. It was an exciting moment for me, knowing that I was heading for command of a ballistic missile submarine on patrol

My Blue crew counterpart was Commander Warren Kelley, a top-notch skipper, well regarded in the force. Warren and I quickly established a close friendship, and five days after arriving on Guam, I took command for my first patrol as skipper. With the Blue crew gone, we settled into the ten-day upkeep routine, during which we prepared the boat for patrol.

Midway through the upkeep, we received orders to get all systems ready for sea, and to sortie when ready for evasion of a typhoon that was heading for Guam. At 2330 that same evening, I reported ready for sea to our squadron commander, Captain Pat Hannifin, and at midnight, we got underway and proceeded out into the Pacific. The shelf drops off steeply around Guam, permitting a submarine to submerge shortly after clearing the entrance channel. We dived the boat, and at 300 feet depth, we prepared to ride out the typhoon, which was forecast to pass within 48 hours. The next morning, however, the weather report stated that the typhoon had stalled and had hardly moved during the past 24 hours. For reasons known only to the gods of storms and perhaps to the weathermen, the typhoon sat in the same locale for the next 48 hours or so before finally beginning lateral movement across the ocean, heading again for Guam. The next day, we began to experience a mild roll, indicating that the seas above were experiencing the growing fury of the storm.

Every evening when at sea, before turning in for the night, a captain writes his night orders which tell the officer of the deck what course, speed, etc., to maintain during the night, as well as standard admonitions regarding standing a taut watch, and calling the CO under certain circumstances, etc. It was approaching 2200, and having just finished writing the night orders, I was entering my room when suddenly, the boat started a rapid ascent, causing a rapid increase in rolls as we went upward into the stormy waters. I fought my way back to the control room, where the young diving officer of the watch was frozen, not knowing what was causing our ascent and thus undecided as to what action to take. The officer of the deck was trying to claw his way forward from the sonar room where he had gone to check on a possible contact. I grabbed the 1MC mike and announced that I had the conn. I then ordered the engines ahead flank, full dive on the planes, and flooding of the ballast tanks. By this time we were taking heavy rolls that were causing people to lose their footing, dishes to crash, and loose gear to be flung about.

After what seemed like a long minute, we felt the boat begin to descend, and now it was gaining depth rapidly. The ballast tanks were pumped, speed was reduced to one-third, we leveled off at a much deeper depth than before, and began to assess the damage. Other than a number of broken dishes, and the ruination of the mid-rations the cooks had been preparing, there was little damage, and no one had sustained any injuries, a small miracle.

Two days later we returned to port, where I reported our adventure, first to the squadron commander, and then to the meteorologists at Andersen Air Force Base. The latter were intrigued by my report, and after studying the conditions found at sea that night, informed me that the stalling of the storm for several days had caused the energy from the wind blowing in the same direction to build up a deep wave similar to a tsunami, and that had picked up our 8500 ton submarine as if it were a surfboard..

We completed our upkeep and got underway for patrol, submerging as soon as we cleared the sea buoy. We were descending to ordered depth when there suddenly was heard a loud buzzing noise that seemed to be coming from an external object that was crossing back and forth above us. While most of those in the control room maintained expressionless faces, I caught several quick smirks and concluded that the crew was trying to play a joke on the new CO, and was waiting to see what the rookie CO would do.

I picked up the 1MC mike: "This is the captain. Rig for ultra quiet." Rigging for ultra quiet requires turning off all air-conditioners, no music or other noise, all hands not on watch to get into bunks, and overall a condition that quickly becomes decidedly uncomfortable in the warm waters of that part of the Pacific. The looks on the faces of the crew clearly indicated that they had not expected that result, and suddenly the noise ceased, with sonar reporting that there were no contacts in the vicinity, other than the ubiquitous Soviet trawler that routinely monitored the arrival and departure of our SSBNs.

In the early years of SSBN strategic patrols, and by this I mean the period from the George Washington's first patrol until the commissioning of the much larger Ohio class in the 1980's, the life of the assigned crews was fairly well predictable, with the approximately 90 days on the boat followed by 90 days of off-crew status at the home port.

The off-crew period was mainly occupied with departure of about one-sixth of the crew and the simultaneous arrival of their replacements, training of officers and enlisted, and short leaves for those who could be spared and who requested leave. Boats home-ported at Pearl Harbor were provided offices and classrooms on Ford Island, the island in the center of Pearl Harbor, which isolated us from the busy hubbub of the naval base. The air station that had been on Ford Island prior to and during the war was no longer in use, providing ready-made buildings for our use.

Included in the training was the annual free ascent from the bottom of a column of water contained in a cylindrical tower, the column being about 120 feet in depth. An annular ring wrapped around the base of the tower, and into this ring crowded those who were about to make the ascent. A vertical door, some four feet by two feet allowed entry into the column of water, but to do so, the air pressure in the ring had to be increased to equal the water pressure at the bottom of the column, in order for the door to be opened. This was done by flooding water into the ring, and as the water level rose, the air above it was compressed. The level of the door was about at the chest level of a six foot man, and the volume of the ring was designed so that when the air pressure in the ring was equal to the water pressure on the other side of the door, the door was under water in the ring. Taking a deep breath, the man about to ascend ducked his head under water, and grasping the interior top of the door frame, pulled himself through the door into the column, being careful not to hit the frame with his head. Once inside the column, he inflated the Mae West life jacket he was wearing and began the ascent.

As he ascended, the compressed air he had inhaled in the ring began to expand in his lungs, and continued to expand all the way up, since the water pressure continually decreased as he ascended. This required him to blow continuously during the ascent, in order to prevent the expanding air in his lungs from rupturing them. As a safety measure, therefore, divers were stationed at 20 feet intervals of depth, and if no bubbles were issuing from a man's mouth, the diver would grab him until he again started blowing. By the time a man reached the top or surface of the column, he had accelerated such that he shot out of the water. Atop the column was an open space with a deck around the bottom and an elevator on one side, on which the one who had ascended could then return to the bottom and the world outside.

At the end of the off-crew period, the crew was flown by chartered flight to Andersen Air Force Base on Guam, and then taken by bus to the tender where we would berth until the Blue crew departed, at which time we moved aboard the boat. The first five days were spent working with the Blue crew, testing equipment and getting a rundown on anything needing repair. On the morning of the sixth day, both crews assembled on the missile deck aft of the sail, attired in dress uniform, and a short but formal change of command took place, and the Blue crew filed off with their personal gear and boarded the bus for the flight home. The next ten days were spent readying the boat for the upcoming patrol, but there usually was time in the evening to go to the Navy club, dubbed the Top O' the Mar, or the club at Andersen, for a dinner and some drinks.

At the appointed date and time, the boat got underway, and submerged when clear of the sea buoy. Barring any unforeseen emergency, we would not surface again until just before arriving near the sea buoy at the end of the patrol, a period of time lasting from 65 to 75 days. My longest patrol was 82 days, caused by our being extended to cover for a boat that had experienced a major engineering plant problem.

The time during the patrol was spent in qualifications on the various ship systems by those working to gain their dolphins as well as those already qualified in submarines who were new to the boat. There were also recreational activities, including evening movies and competition in various games such as bridge, checkers, chess, acey-deucey, poker, and a special team competition conducted near the end of the patrol in which teams took turns doing the voices of movies that had been seen a number of times during the patrol. For the movie competition, the sound was turned off, and as the movie rolled, the team members said the parts of the various actors, or tried to, with some hilarious results at times. The XO, the COB and I were the judges and the winners got a case of beer when we returned to Pearl. This turned into the most popular extra-curricular activity on board, and the COB and the XO had to formulate some strict rules for the competition, such as limiting the number of times a team could view the film they had chosen For the more intellectual members, there was a small but well-stocked library. I enjoyed reading, but always entered the acey-deucey tournament, and even won the championship on one patrol.

Constant reception of message traffic while submerged was maintained by use of a floating wire antenna about the thickness of a finger that streamed out behind the boat. While on patrol, we had to be ready to launch our missiles within a short period of time, so it was necessary for us to be receiving an unbroken stream of messages during the entire patrol, that being the means by which we would receive a launch order from the president. At least twice on every patrol, we would receive an emergency action message (EAM) that was authentic in every detail but lacked an actual launch order. We had to spin up the missiles, and complete other steps for rigging Condition 1M.

We were constantly alert for the presence of another submarine, and took measures to check for their presence, being careful not to do so at regular intervals or to use the same methods repeatedly. It was a game of hide and seek, with the missile carrying submarine always "it." If a Soviet attack boat could locate us and then trail us, he could preempt a launch of our missiles by sinking us with a torpedo if the call for war ever came. In order for us to remain a credible threat we had to remain undetected. It was the ability of our force to in fact avoid detection that provided the leverage needed to prevent a hot war, the possible use of nuclear weapons being a strong deterrent.

We had completed the fourth patrol under my command and were in the midst of the off-crew routine when we learned that the Kam was being transferred to the Atlantic Fleet upon the return of the Blue crew, who would be bringing the boat into Pearl Harbor instead of Guam.

The Kamehameha understandably held a special place in the hearts of the people of Hawaii, and when Kam came in from her last Pacific patrol, she was met by a delegation of top level politicians and businessmen, who placed a huge lei over the front of the sail. The Gold crew was drawn up in ranks, and gave the traditional three cheers for their comrades in the Blue crew.

After relieving the Blue crew, we spent the next three weeks preparing for the trip to Charleston, including making arrangements for the shipping of household effects for all the married personnel. The latter was handled so well by the executive officer, Lieutenant Commander Frank Meredith, that the boat received a message of commendation from the Commandant of the Fourteenth Naval District.

We also were tasked with making short cruises for local VIPs, On one such, we were accompanied by a young female reporter from the Honolulu Star-Bulletin. During the short cruise, she interviewed me as well as several of the crew. She took notes as I emphasized the important mission of a ballistic missile submarine, and the deterrent role it played in keeping the Cold War cold. The next morning, as I scanned the newspaper, I was chagrined to find her story on the Women's page of the Society section. The whole article was devoted to describing what it was like to be in a submerged submarine, surrounded by all those good-looking men, including the captain, who was described as being "deeply tanned, with sea blue eyes." The last paragraph did briefly mention that the boat played an important role in the Cold War.

When I arrived at the Kam's berth at the Submarine Base, the crew was assembled on deck, holding a large sign that read, "We wish we had sea blue eyes."

The Gold crew of the Kamehameha was the best group of sailors and officers that a captain could ever have. In three years of command, I did not have a single disciplinary case, an experience rarely seen. After seeing their superb performance on the first two patrols, I decided that they deserved something special, so I conferred with the XO and the Chief of the Boat, and asked them if they thought a suitable gesture would be to have a Captain's Dinner during our return trip from patrol during which each man would receive a can of cold beer. Navy regulations prohibit the carrying or serving of alcoholic beverages on board Navy vessels, except for small bottles of brandy to be used only for medicinal purposes. The XO reminded me of that fact, and I said I was well aware of it. I looked at the COB, who said the crew would be delighted. So the XO, the COB and I each spirited aboard two cases of beer, stowed in the locker under my bunk. We also had white linen table cloths and silver candle holders brought aboard.

Finally, the third patrol was completed and we were heading back to Guam. The Plan of the Day announced that all hands less watch standers were to be in dress uniforms for the evening meal which was to be strictly on time at 1800 in the Crew's Mess. There was some grumbling about having to get into dress uniforms while still at sea, but when they entered the Crew's Mess, they were stunned into silence at the sight of the white table cloths and the candles. I entered in my dress uniform at 1800, and welcomed all to the Captain's Dinner, filet mignon and apple pie ala mode for dessert, and then in walked the COB, the XO, and a half dozen grinning sailors , carrying the chilled cases of beer. Cheers erupted as the COB and the XO handed each man a cold one. They then gave three cheers for the Kam, and sat down to enjoy the dinner and the beer, with the beer going down first in most cases. The knowledge that they were partaking of forbidden beer made it all the more enjoyable, and knowing the consequences for me if the word got out ashore, no one ever broached the secret, not even to their wives. We continued the practice for the rest of my days in command.

The day we got underway for Charleston, a large crowd of locals were on hand, and we could hear the strains of Aloha Nui floating from the shore as we made our way to sea.

When we arrived at the Pacific side of the Panama Canal, we surfaced and met a boat carrying the canal pilot, who boarded, took the conn, and we immediately commenced our passage through the canal, where priority is given to nuclear submarines. It was an interesting experience for us, with a lot of pictures being snapped from other ships as we passed them. As we entered the Caribbean, we disembarked the pilot, rigged for dive, and down we went, on our way north to Charleston.

The day prior to our arrival, we received a message from Charleston, advising us of the arrangements for our entry, including the promise that Miss Charleston would be on the tug bringing the pilot.

The next morning, we surfaced at the appointed time, just east of the sea buoy marking the entrance to the channel, a location with which I was familiar from my tour in minesweepers. I would have had no trouble bringing Kam into port, but our instructions were to await the arrival of the pilot before proceeding into the channel, so we slowed to three knots, and loitered in the vicinity of the sea buoy. The officer of the deck and the junior officer of the deck were both bachelors, and were eagerly looking forward to meeting and escorting Miss Charleston, and both kept a sharp scan for the pilot boat. Soon a craft appeared and came alongside, but it was bearing a reporter and photographer from the Charleston Courier. I invited them up to the bridge, and they told us that a Navy tug was not far behind them

"There it is, sir, coming out the channel, and there is a woman on it!"

All eyes swiveled in the direction of the channel, and almost immediately, there came the report from the OOD, with an audible tone of disgust:

"Captain, that isn't Miss Charleston, that's your wife!"

Sure enough, there was my smiling bride, waving happily to all of us, but there was no Miss Charleston. We later learned that she had gone to the wrong place and had missed the boat, literally.

The next day's newspaper gleefully headlined the comment of the young OOD, with the accompanying article being a parody of the old joke, "That's no lady, that's my wife."

The third day after our arrival, I was summoned to the office of Rear Admiral Shannon Cramer, the commander of the Charleston submarine group, Submarine Flotilla Six. Admiral Cramer was one of the finest officers in the Navy, and had an outstanding reputation, especially within the submarine community.

"Jim, one of our deploying SSBNs has suffered a major casualty in the engineering plant and won't be able to make its patrol. Can your boat change all sixteen missiles and be ready to get underway within 36 hours?"

"Yes sir, we can do that."

"How soon can you get up the Cooper River to the missile handling facility?"

"In four hours, sir."

"Alright, make it so, and when you are nearing completion of the missile exchange, give me a call, and I'll go out with you for a short sea trial before you deploy."

"Aye aye, sir."

I hurried down to the Kam, and had the XO call in all those who were taking some liberty in order to help their families to get settled in their new quarters. This took about an hour, and in the meantime, I informed the engineers that we would be getting underway in three hours, and alerted the weapons department of the missile exchange. The supply officer was told to get stores aboard while we were at the missile facility, and the navigator was told to get the charts for the Atlantic and the Mediterranean, since we could be going to either for the patrol. We all had the feeling of "Welcome to the Atlantic Fleet."

As promised, we made the missile exchange without any problems, completing it in less than twenty hours, and got underway with Admiral Cramer and Captain Will Adams, our squadron commander, on board. I had the conn, and we proceeded down the Cooper River, and on out the channel.

We spent the next four days running through drills for the admiral, and then headed back into Charleston, arriving about midnight. I took the conn when we entered the channel, and took the boat through the harbor and up the river to the submarine base. Admiral Cramer was on the bridge, observing our maneuvering as we wended our way to the base. I later learned that many submarine skippers, especially those with limited surface experience, had had difficulty navigating into Charleston at night, due mostly to confusion about the various lights that were the aids to navigation at night. The squadron commander told me that Admiral Cramer had described our shiphandling and navigation "in glowing terms," which just illustrates how much fate has a way of shaping things .My knowledge of Charleston harbor from my days in minesweepers gave me an advantage not enjoyed by the other skippers.

Kam received a single-page sailing order in lieu of the standard multi-page patrol oporder, in which Commander Submarine Flotilla Six directed Kam to proceed to a designated point in the ocean a short distance from the base at Rota, Spain where we were to meet a fleet tug that would deliver our necessary orders for the patrol.

We surfaced off of Rota, in a heavy fog, and commenced sounding fog signals. Soon, we heard another ship's fog horn, and out of the heavy mist appeared our tug. Within a few minutes, we had the oilskin package delivered by the tug and were on our way back out to deep water.

After submerging, the XO, the navigator and I opened the package, and it was then we learned that we would be making the patrol in the Mediterranean.

The Atlantic is colder in temperature than the waters of the Mediterranean, causing the colder Atlantic water to flow into the Mediterranean underneath the outflow of the warmer water from the Med. During the Second World War, U-boats had used this deeper inflowing current to take them into the Med to avoid detection by the listening stations at the Strait of Gibraltar. We also took advantage of the inflowing current and commenced our Med patrol.

A Med patrol is far different from a patrol in the open spaces of the Pacific or Atlantic. The sea space is limited and is shared with a heavy ship traffic that is never light. Adding to the possible risks is the continuous passage of deep draft tankers, whose draft is such that the screw rides deep, thus there is little to no cavitation, so sonar has difficulty in hearing them and identifying them.

One evening, the navigator informed me that we needed to get a star sight, used to correct the small errors that had crept into the ship's inertial navigation system. We slowly ascended to periscope depth, listening carefully for any sign of a ship nearby. At one hundred feet, I raised the periscope and commenced slowly sweeping through a full circle, looking for any phosphorescence that would be caused by the passage of the ship in the plankton floating in the water. As I rotated the scope to the left, I saw what appeared to be a phosphorescent V, heading toward us off our port bow. I ordered "down scope, ahead full, depth steady, steady as you go."

After a run of a minute or so, I slowed to patrol speed and came left ninety degrees. Sonar now reported hearing engine noises passing down our port side. We ascended to periscope depth, where the navigator then obtained his star fix, and we proceeded back to patrol depth without any further incidents. After our return to homeport, I learned that such an encounter with a deep draft ship was a common occurrence in the Med.

As our patrol ended, we headed for the Strait of Gibraltar, and this time, we went to periscope depth as we rode the outflow in the warm upper current as it streamed into the Atlantic. Once clear of the strait, we went deep, and the dramatic change in water temperature and salinity, colder temperature, less salinity, required some work by the diving officer of the watch to get us in trim again. We set course for Charleston, and increased speed to our "go-home" speed.

When we surfaced a mile or so east of the sea buoy, we were met by a tug bearing ComSubFlot Six, RADM Shannon Cramer, who congratulated the crew on their outstanding performance, a tribute they had certainly earned.

We made one more patrol, this time in the Atlantic, a routine patrol with no encounters such as the one we had in the Med. Upon return to Charleston , the Gold crew was relieved by the Blue crew, who then took Kamehameha into the shipyard for a major overhaul. I had completed six patrols on Kam, and was detached without relief, the Gold crew having been disbanded for the year or so the boat was in the yard. Saying farewell to my XO, Frank Meredith, was especially hard. All of the officers and the crew had performed superbly, but it was Frank who was my steady anchor and who oversaw the day to day operations that ran so smoothly.

Concurrent with promotion to captain came orders to the Pentagon, a tour that I had hoped to avoid.

15

The Pentagon, July 1971

My orders to the Pentagon were the result of my prior association with Stan Turner, who was now a rear admiral in charge of OP-96, the systems analysis division of the staff of the Chief of Naval Operations, Admiral Zumwalt. OP-96 was a part of OP-090, the Director, Navy Program Planning, Vice Admiral Worth Bagley. It was newly established, and was the Navy's answer to the constant intrusions into Navy planning and programming by the Assistant Secretary of Defense for Systems Analysis. It enjoyed a high level of importance within OpNav, and was given high priority in assignment of officers.

I was assigned as head of the Anti-Submarine Warfare section of the Sea Control Group, and after three months, I was moved up to head of the Sea Control Group. In the latter assignment, my principal task was to develop a new approach to planning and programming called the CNO Program Alternatives Memorandum, CPAM for short.

The purpose of the CPAM was to give the CNO alternative options to programs submitted by the three Deputy Chiefs of Naval Operations who were responsible for surface warfare, submarine warfare, and aviation warfare. This approach initially was not popular among the warfare czars who saw it as a way of criticizing their programs with possible loss of the programs or causing major changes over which they had no control. However, once they were briefed by us and saw that our only intent was to assist them in perhaps improving their programs, they supported the approach, and the CPAM became a regular part of the process at that time. However, our office was under pressure from the lower OpNav echelons to support their respective submissions, pressures that we necessarily could not accommodate since doing so would defeat the purpose of the CPAM.

After a year in OP-96, I was assigned as deputy director of the CNO Executive Panel, a group of five officers personally selected by Admiral Zumwalt, including the director, Rear Admiral Kinnaird McKee, and three commanders, Tom Brooks, a naval intelligence specialist, Bill Miller, and Bill Dougherty. Tom Brooks later served as Director of Naval Intelligence, Bill Miller was Chief of Naval Research and later was Dean of Academics at the Naval Academy, and Bill Dougherty retired a vice admiral. Kin McKee eventually rose to four star rank and relieved Admiral Rickover as head of Naval Reactors.

The purpose of the CEP was to provide professional support to the group of prominent civilians, leaders in their respective fields, whom the CNO had appointed to be his advisors as required from time to time, in which capacity they served on a voluntary basis. In addition, the CEP staff was used by the CNO for various special tasks.

One such task for me was a visit to the naval warfare section in CIA for a discussion of their analysis of a certain Soviet weapons system. I was dismayed to find that the analysts were several young recent college graduates who had no first-hand knowledge of navies, having never served in any branch of the armed forces, let alone the Navy. Their analysis was based on information from reading attaché reports, as well as books by various authors who specialized in naval subjects.

I was especially disturbed by their attitude, namely, because they were CIA, they considered that theirs was the final word on the analysis of a specific item. In the case of the Soviet weapon system under discussion, they had no concept of the possible effect of the system on our tactics in warfare at sea. Their analysis of the Soviet weapon system was, in my opinion, shallow and incomplete, and I so reported to the CNO.

I was only with the CEP five months when I was ordered to relieve Captain Bob Monroe as executive secretary of the CNO Executive Board, OP-090X, working for Vice Admiral Worth Bagley for whom it was a pleasure to work, and an officer for whom I had and have the deepest respect and regard. The CNO Executive Board was chaired by the CNO, and included the Vice CNO, and the three star officers in OpNav. Its purpose was to evaluate program proposals, and to consider any other items as selected by the CNO or proposed by any of the members. My task was to screen items for the CEB, and if selected by the CNO for a CEB meeting, to notify the members and schedule the CEB as early as possible.

I also was tasked to review proposals and submit a point paper, in which I expressed my analysis.

It was in the latter capacity that I found myself reviewing a proposal from Admiral Rickover for an "Advanced High Performance Nuclear Attack Submarine."

The AHPSSN was Admiral Rickover's response to the Charlie class Soviet nuclear submarine. His intent was to construct a nuclear submarine that could match the Charlie's speed but would remain quiet at the top speed, unlike the Charlie which was very noisy. The quieting feature required a large hull volume, and would considerably increase the cost of the submarine. The Navy had just begun building the SSN-688 class to replace the 637 class, and it was apparent that the money needed for the AHPSSN would drain funds from the 688 program. I asked a member of Rickover's staff what weapons the AHPSSN would carry, and was told that it would be a SSGN, carrying missiles as well as torpedoes. The Navy had yet to develop a guided missile that could be launched from a submarine, but I was assured by the Rickover staffer that such a missile was forthcoming. While it was true that the Navy was in the concept phase of planning for such a missile, its development would take a number of years that left the AHPSSN with torpedoes only. I also raised the issue of cost and its impact on the 688 program, and was assured that Rickover would be able to persuade Congress to fully fund both, a promise that I doubted could be fulfilled.

My point paper to the CNO recommended disapproval of the AHPSSN for the reasons mentioned. At the ensuing CEB. the proposal was disapproved, and I went to the head of Admiral Rickover's black list.

I had a year of obligated service remaining in the rank of captain before I could request retirement. Aware of my standing with Admiral Rickover, I decided that I would retire when eligible and would attend law school to pursue a second career in law. I took the LSAT examination, and was accepted at American and George Washington universities, but not at Georgetown. With the children all in college or high school, Peggy had obtained a license as a real estate agent, and was working for a firm in Potomac, Maryland, so I applied only at the local law schools.

Shortly after I had accepted entry at American, I was notified one afternoon that Vice Admiral Eugene Wilkinson, the head of submarine warfare on the OpNav staff, wished to see me in his office. When I entered, he invited me to be seated, and then said, "What are we going to do with you?"

I replied, "Not a problem, Admiral." I then told him of my plans to retire and attend law school.

"No, you are not."

"Yes, sir, I am."

"No, you are not," he repeated, pointing at his three-star shoulder boards. "Here is what you are going to do. First of all, you know that Admiral Rickover has down-checked every submarine command we have proposed for you, and if you are to be eligible for promotion to flag rank, you have to have successfully completed a major command tour, either afloat or ashore. Now, you went to Naval Intelligence School, and the Naval Intelligence Command has just set up a major command over in Suitland, called the Naval Intelligence Support Center, and the CO billet calls for a submarine officer with command experience. That's where you are going, because it will be a billet over which Admiral Rickover has no say, and it will fill the requirement for major command."

Two weeks later, I assumed command of NISC, which employed over 600 civilian analysts and some 200 naval personnel. The work in which they were engaged was fascinating. I also found that little of their results were reaching those in the Navy who needed to know, the senior leaders and planners.

My tour as executive secretary of the CNO Executive Board had necessarily placed me in near daily contact with the executive assistants of the admirals in the E-Ring of the Pentagon, and I called each of them, offering to brief their principals either in their office or at NISC. At first, the response was slow, but after briefing several, the word quickly spread that NISC had valuable intelligence to impart, and soon we were briefing the Vice Chief and the CNO, who then directed that I go out to the fleet commands and brief them, which I did. All of this took place in the period of May 1974 to February 1975.

In October, 1974, the Director of Naval Intelligence, Vice Admiral Rectanus, directed me to visit my counterparts in the several navies of NATO, less Greece and Turkey. Peggy accompanied me, but at our expense.

Our tour began with the United Kingdom, where we were met in London by then Captain John Robertson, RN, and his lovely wife, Kathleen, who hosted us during our stay in London. John retired as a rear admiral, and he and Kathleen have remained two of my favorite people. After meetings with the Royal Navy's intelligence activities, Peggy and I entrained for Wales, to visit the sound listening station at Pembroke, commanded by my classmate, Captain Bob Jacob. We had to change trains at Cardiff, and we were joined in our compartment by a gentleman who sat down opposite Peggy. He said something to her, and she said, "Pardon me?" He repeated what he had said, and Peggy said, "I am sorry, I speak only English."

In a somewhat exasperated tone, the gentleman said, in a very heavy Welsh accent and very slowly, "Madame, I am speaking English!"

My unfazed bride laughed, obviously laughing at herself, said she was sorry, and was delighted to meet a Welshman. A broad smile was her reward, and they chatted the rest of the trip

We stayed in a charming inn at Pembroke, and enjoyed having high tea at 4 pm with crumpets and hard cream. That evening Bob and Nancy Jacob took us to a pub where the locals treated us to their beautiful Welsh singing. The next morning, Bob picked me up, and gave me a tour of the facility he commanded.

Then very early the following morning it was off to London, by train, and a flight from Heathrow to Leonardo Da Vinci airport, near

Rome. We visited Rome, and then traveled on to Naples, for more briefings for me. We were treated to dinner by the McKees, Kin being stationed at Naples at that time, commanding the submarine group.

Next stop was Copenhagen. The attaché had reserved a room at a small hotel, behind which, very close by, ran a railroad. We received a noisy massage about every two hours as trains went rattling by while we attempted to sleep.

My Danish colleagues gave a traditional all-male dinner for me at which I received the traditional skoal toasts and speeches. The only one I recall was the one where the speaker told this story. He began by remarking that it was not my fault that I was of Swedish ancestry, for which he and his fellow Danes felt pity for me. Then followed the tale of a shipload of Scandinavians who were wrecked on a deserted island. After getting ashore, the Danes immediately started a cooperative, and after seeing that it was working, the Norwegians joined it. But the poor Swedes starved to death because they were waiting to be introduced. I was tempted to ask why they let the poor Swedes starve, but thought it best to forego the question.

The final stop was Oslo, Norway, where the attaché, a fellow submariner, took me up to the North Cape, the northernmost part of Europe. The trees there are stunted and hard as iron due to their very small growth rate, caused by the climate and lack of sunlight. This is the land of the Lapland people, who are not of the same genetic origin as the Scandinavians. They subsist largely on reindeer, which they have domesticated, using every part of the animals much as the Native Americans used the buffalo. Their clothing is bright red and blue wool, very warm and comfortable.

We returned to Dulles via London, flying on SAS. When we unpacked at home, Peggy discovered that her bag had been rifled and her charm bracelet had been stolen, most likely during our layover at Heathrow. The charms had been collected over the years and were irreplaceable.

It was the spring of 1975, Rear Admiral Bobby R. Inman was the Director of Naval Intelligence, and Admiral James L. Holloway, III, was the Chief of Naval Operations. I was seated at my desk at the Naval Intelligence Support Center on a late afternoon, catching up on paperwork when the door opened and in came Admiral Inman, unannounced. Before I could stand, he was at my desk, and extending his hand, he said, "Congratulations! You're on the flag selection list that just came out!"

I was stunned. After my experience with Admiral Rickover, I had given up any thought of making flag, and was looking forward to starting law school later that year, after retiring from the Navy. Inman shook my hand and left.

I called Peggy and told her the news, and then I called my brother, who was more excited by the news than I was. By now, the word had sped throughout NISC, and I was besieged by those who wished to extend their congratulations. I thanked them all, and headed for home, feeling as if I was floating. I was still having trouble comprehending it all, but as it sank in, I realized that much more was ahead for me in my beloved Navy.

16

First Flag Duty

On 29 May 1975, I turned over command of NISC to Captain Bob Lumsden, a classmate and fellow submariner. Immediately following the change of command, I donned the uniform of a rear admiral and reported to Admiral Inman as Deputy Director of Naval Intelligence. Working for and with Bob Inman was a true pleasure. We had been fellow students at Naval Intelligence School when we were lieutenants, and Peggy and I had attended his wedding to Nancy, a lovely native of the District of Columbia. Bob had transferred to the intelligence corps, and had been assigned as assistant naval attaché in Stockholm. His personal brilliance quickly established him as the top naval intelligence officer of his rank, a reputation that grew with the years, culminating in his early selection for flag rank and his immediate assignment as Director of Naval Intelligence. He ultimately retired in the rank of admiral, and was the Deputy Director of the Central Intelligence Agency, following a very successful tour as Director of the National Security Agency. He was particularly adept in his relations with the members of Congress, and enjoyed their highest respect and admiration.

The year I spent as DDNI went by quickly, marked by frequent social gatherings with the naval attaches of the embassies in Washington. One such was a football game at RFK Stadium with the Washington Redskins playing Dallas. I escorted the Soviet attaché, who was a captain first rank and a nuclear submariner, a tie that transcended our political differences, although we still were careful not to make our personal connection too close. My Soviet comrade was not familiar with American football, so I tried to explain what was happening. He was impressed by the roughness of the game, and the game itself he likened to a form of combat. But what intrigued him most was the high school marching band that performed at half-time. He could not believe that the youngsters were just high school students, because they played and marched so well.

In March of 1976, I was called to the office of the Vice CNO, Admiral Hal Shear, a submariner. He informed me that I was being ordered to command of the South Atlantic Force, based at Roosevelt Roads, Puerto Rico. He explained that the principal task of ComSoLant was to conduct the annual UNITAS exercise with the navies of South America, an exercise that was in its seventeenth year. (At that time, there were two sea commands maintained for special purposes, one being the South Atlantic Force, and the other being the Middle East Force, based at Bahrain, in the Persian Gulf, a ready force to protect the flow of oil out of the Gulf. The former is now the US Fourth Fleet, while the latter is the Fifth Fleet.). Admiral Shear further informed me that, during UNITAS XVI, one of our vessels had collided with a merchant ship while approaching the Panama Canal on the Caribbean side of the canal. He described it as an embarrassment to the US Navy, and cautioned me to exercise care to ensure that there would be no similar incidents. Finally, he told me that I was to accompany Rear Admiral George Ellis, the current ComSoLant, for at least part of the planning trip to South America, during which the staff worked with the various navies of our neighbor continent in planning the schedule for our visits to their countries.

So I flew to Roosevelt Roads in a P-3 from the squadron based in Maine, the same aircraft in which we would be flying to South America. After an overnight in Roosevelt Roads, we flew to Cartagena, Colombia, then to Lima, Peru, and then to Valparaiso, Chile. It was in Chile that I was given a lesson in the diversity that exists among the countries of South America, unlike the North American image of all below the border being more or less the same.

The planning conference in Chile was held in Viña del Mar, the seaside resort for Valparaiso. After the afternoon siesta, I walked the mile or so from our hotel to the shopping area, where I bought several items. Since I now had a load of packages, I decided to take the bus back to the hotel, so I stepped into the nearest shop and asked the proprietor, "¿ Por favor, señor, dónde está la parada?" (Please, sir, where is the bus stop?) The man looked at me with a quizzical frown, and said, "¿Como, señor?" (What, sir?) I repeated the question. He then said in very broken English, "Are you American?" "Yes," I replied. "Do you know what means parada?" I said , "Bus stop?" "No, señor," he replied, "it is what you put on the baby!" I was asking him where the diaper was! This was my first lesson in learning that the same word can have very different meanings from country to country, somewhat like what Americans call an elevator being called a "lift" in England. Parada is the usual Spanish word for bus stop, derived from the verb parar, to stop, but in Chile, a bus stop is the estación de autobus, shortened to estación.

I flew back to Washington from Chile.

The UNITAS exercises served several purposes, namely, to show the flag in support of good relations with the countries of South America; to provide a means for developing contacts that would be useful to us and to them in the event of a conflict in which we were defending the Western Hemisphere; and to evaluate the ability of our Navy to work effectively with the South Americans. Therefore, the schedule was a mixture of port visits with attendant social activities, and exercises at sea with the navy of the host country. Since it was 1976, the 200th anniversary of the Declaration of Independence, the schedule varied from the norm, in that the ships of the Force would assemble at Ft. Lauderdale, where we would be joined by a Brazilian destroyer and a Chilean frigate, in tribute to the anniversary. The schedule also included a stop in the Caribbean at the site of the first salute to the flag of the American united colonies.

Here, let me turn to some family history, and then I shall return to the Navy.

Near the end of my tour as DDNI, Peggy had decided that we should move from our home on Democracy Lane in Potomac, Maryland, due to the large increase in population that had occurred over the past five years of our residence there. We looked at several places in Georgetown, and had placed a contract on an 18th century house in Old Town Alexandria that fell through when the realtor representing the seller decided that the house should go to a friend of his. Our agent wanted to sue him, but we were not enchanted at the prospect of long days in court.

Then, one Sunday, after Mass, Peggy told me she had found a place out in the countryside of Virginia, and as we drove and drove out US Route 50 West, I began to wonder just what she was getting us into. About five miles west of Middleburg, she turned south onto County Route 713, and we drove through large horse farms that were beautifully groomed. Some three miles later, we entered the village of Rectortown, and continued south another quarter mile or so where, on the south side of the village, she turned into the driveway of a large white frame house that stood atop a hill about 100 yards off the road. The house was named Maidstone, and was built for Harriet Rector when she married in 1850. Sitting on a wooded lot of about two acres, the house had a small barn on the north side of the lot, and a two story detached garage on the east edge of the lot, behind the house at the end of a gravel driveway. The house faced the Blue Ridge, which was about three miles to the west. The house contained five bedrooms, two of which were in a wing that had been added in the 1940s, three and a half baths, a large living room, a large dining room, and a kitchen with heavy dark wood cupboards. Behind the kitchen was a detached one room cottage, connected by a short covered walk, built for the nurse of a previous owner, Roland Pierce, who had been the president of the Marshall National Bank in nearby Marshall, Virginia. Mr. Pierce suffered from emphysema, and was unable to climb the stairs.

We bought Maidstone in late May 1976, and in June I reported for duty as ComSoLant, at Roosevelt Roads, on the east coast of Puerto Rico.

I should mention here that Mark, who was entering his junior year at Winston Churchill High School in Potomac, stayed in Potomac and was boarding with Ruth and Jim Hay who also lived in Potomac and whose son, Jeff, was a close friend and classmate of Mark. Jim was a submariner, captain, Naval Academy class of 1954, and worked for the Director, Net Assessment in the office of the Secretary of Defense. Jim and Ruth are wonderful people, who readily "adopted" Mark. Jeannine was entering her freshman year at Auburn. Denise, after a year at Mt. St. Mary's in Emmitsburg, Maryland, had transferred to Florida State and was going into her junior year. Lisa spent her college freshman year at Georgetown University's School of Foreign Service, and then transferred to Florida State, from which she graduated in 1975 with honors in International Relations. After spending a year in Hawaii selling seeds to save the Manoa Valley, Lisa joined us in Puerto Rico and was working at the Officers Club at Roosevelt Roads, where we were quartered. Denise and Jeannine both graduated from Winston Churchill.

Upon completion of her junior year at FSU, Lisa went to Switzerland to spend the summer in a work program she had signed on for. She had expected to be assigned to the French speaking sector but instead found herself in Meiringen, in the German sector, working in a restaurant with a girl from Canada and one from England. They were quartered in a hut up the hill behind the restaurant, and worked and lived in rather rugged conditions. With not much to do other than work, the three saved their wages and at the end of the summer, took off on a hitchhiking tour of western Europe. The first we learned of their tour was when we received a postcard from Paris, showing a view of the bridges along the Seine near Notre Dame, and an arrow pointing to a spot under a bridge with the note, "This is where I slept last night."

To say that her mother was upset would be an understatement. Peggy was ready to fly to France, but I noted that by the time she arrived in Paris, our nomadic daughter would be somewhere else in Europe, so Peggy stayed home, blitzing Heaven with her prayers. Then a card arrived from Belgium, informing us that the three were going to England to spend several days with the family of the English girl, and then she would be flying home.

Some days later, the phone rang, and it was our peripatetic perambulator, informing us that she was at Dulles, and would we please come pick her up. Given Peggy's penchant for jumping into adventures, I could not understand why she did not understand the same impulse in her daughter. Maybe she did, but worried just the same. In any event, she was so happy to see Lisa, there were no recriminations. On the way home, Lisa informed us that she had spent her last twenty-five cents making the call to us. Now that takes very careful planning!

As we prepared to move to Puerto Rico, Denise and Jeannine had arranged to stay with friends from Winston Churchill, and Denise informed us that she had obtained a job for the summer at Wolf Trap, the entertainment center outside Washington, located in northern Virginia. I asked Jeannine what she was going to do, and she burst into tears, because she had not yet had any success at getting work for the summer. Big sister Denise told her not to worry, and got her a job also at Wolf Trap. Mark and Jeff Hay had all the work they could handle, mowing lawns in the area. So when we arrived in Puerto Rico, we were without three of our nestlings, but had regained one.

17

Commander, South Atlantic Force, U.S. Atlantic Fleet

Shortly after relieving Rear Admiral Ellis as ComSoLant, I embarked with my staff in the P-3 aircraft and flew to Ft. Lauderdale, Florida. Because it was 1976, the 200th anniversary of the Declaration of Independence, the South Atlantic Force was gathering in a port of one of the states rather than rendezvousing at sea on the way to South America. The Force usually consisted of a DLG, a DD and a smaller frigate, together with a nuclear attack submarine, two P-3 aircraft, a Navy transport aircraft, and the CincLantFlt Show Band. The latter flew in the Navy transport. At some earlier point in time, someone decided that it was good practice in promoting good relations to have Mrs. ComSoLant accompany the cruise via the Navy transport, so special authorization was given for Mrs. CSL to ride in that specific aircraft for the purpose of promoting good will, provided all hotel and food expenses were personally paid for by Mrs. CSL. Peggy was given a crash course in Spanish by the State Department, and during the course of UNITAS XVII, she visited a number of inland towns, traveling with the show band that performed at those towns while we were at sea conducting exercises with the host navy.

On the way from Ft. Lauderdale to South America, we stopped at the tiny island of St. Eustatius, the Dutch island where the first salute to our flag was to be commemorated. The secretary of the Navy,

William Middendorf, was on board, and was slated to speak at the ceremony on the island. There was only a small and rudimentary landing at the island, but we made it ashore from the admiral's barge without mishap. There were several hundred people who lived on St. Eustatius, descendants of slaves, and all were on hand to greet us and to hear Secretary Middendorf's address.

It was sad to see how much those poor people were counting on our visit to somehow put St. Eustatius on the tourist map, an outcome which was hopelessly remote, given the rundown condition of the island, the lack of adequate hotel and entertainment facilities, and the fact that the island totally lacked any visual appeal.

The circumnavigation of South America was alternated, one year being clockwise and the next year counter-clockwise. UNITAS XVII went clockwise, with our first country to be visited being Venezuela, where we made our first call at the port of La Guaira, the port for the capital, Caracas, which is some miles inland. There began the sequence of formal calls on the head of the navy, the fleet commander, and the senior officer commanding the ships with which we would be operating, followed by a wreath-laying ceremony at the statue of the country's chief patriot. I presented each officer with a small gift and a plaque bearing the ComSoLant emblem, and received similar gifts in return. The evening was occupied by a formal reception and dinner hosted by the local navy. The next day, I hosted a formal dinner aboard the flagship, usually followed by a tour of the local sites. This was more or less the routine in port in each country, with some offering additional entertainment such as a night club or theater.

The Navy Show Band performed in a public park during the day, and at the dance that followed the reception and dinner. Peggy was a terrific dancer, and rapidly became a big hit with the host officers. She also accompanied the band as it traveled to various inland towns on their plane while we were at sea conducting exercises with the local navy. She had some interesting experiences during these travels. At one town, the hotel where she and the band were staying had no air conditioning, so Peggy was sitting on the veranda on the front of the hotel, getting some of the evening breeze. Soon she was being visited by one man after another, each of whom spoke to her in Spanish, which she could not understand, and when the men realized she was an American visitor, they quickly departed. It finally dawned on her that she was being mistaken for a lady of the night, and she decided that she had better go back inside, despite the heat.

We usually spent five days at sea for the exercises with the host navy ships, the exercises being conducted by the American destroyer squadron commander who accompanied the ships from his squadron. For UNITAS XVII, the squadron commander was Captain Don McVay, a superb officer who conducted the exercises with exceptional skill, so that all went very smoothly. My staff was well supervised by the chief of staff, Captain Skip Van Dusen. The staff and I observed each drill and evaluated how well it was executed. We kept a comprehensive record of the details of each, which would serve as the source for my report to CincLantFlt after our return to Puerto Rico.

With a few exceptions, we found the navies of South America to be well drilled and capable of executing naval missions expertly and smartly. As might be expected, this was true of all the navies of the larger countries, with the Chilean Navy at the head of the list, closely followed by Brazil, Peru, Argentina, and Venezuela. Brazil and Argentina each had a small aircraft carrier, and all navies had destroyers, frigates, patrol aircraft, helicopters, and a small number of modern diesel submarines, usually the German-built Type 209. Chile, Peru, Argentina and Brazil also had several replenishment ships from which we refueled and reprovisioned at sea. In addition, Chile, Brazil and Argentina had several ex-US light cruisers of World War II vintage. Argentina's cruiser, the Belgrano, was later sunk by a British nuclear submarine during the Falklands War, with heavy loss of life.

As we sailed around the southern continent, we visited the ports of La Guaira and Puerto La Cruz in Venezuela; Fortaleza, Recife, Salvador, and Rio de Janeiro in Brazil; Montevideo, Uruguay; Puerto Belgrano and Puerto Madryn, Argentina; Punta Arenas, Talcahuano, Puerto Montt, Valparaiso, and Puerto Aldea, Chile; Callao and Paita, Peru; and transited the Panama Canal for our last port, Cartagena, Colombia. The entire trip around the continent took about four months, specifically, from 10 July to 21 November 1976. We had arrived in Ft. Lauderdale on 3 July for the observance of the 200th anniversary of the Declaration of Independence, and had departed by ship from there. My flagship was the good ship USS MacDonough (DDG-39), commanded by Commander Rich Beggs, an outstanding officer whose ship reflected his excellent leadership.

Most North Americans think of our neighbors south of us as one Hispanic people, but if they were to travel to South America they would find countries with diverse peoples and diverse customs from country to country and from city to city. In Chile, for example, those who live in Valparaiso and Concepción are every bit as sophisticated and upscale as Parisians or New Yorkers, while the Chilenos who live in the fishing towns of Puerto Montt or Talcahuano are down-to-earth and hardy like their counterparts in New England or Cornwall. Each country has its own traditions and customs, and even the meaning of a word can vary from one country to another. National pride runs deep, perhaps too deep, and Peru and Bolivia, for example, are still smarting from their defeat by Chile in the War of the Pacific that took place in the 1870s.

In early January I traveled to Norfolk to make my report to Admiral Kidd at his CincLantFlt headququarters. The Deputy, and several of the three star type commanders received my briefing and complimented us on the reports they had received from the South American navies regarding our conduct of the operation.

After a brief time at Roosevelt Roads, during which we sketched out plans for the next operation, we boarded our P-3 sent to us from Brunswick, Maine, and set out for our planning tour with the Latin navies. Six weeks later, we returned to Puerto Rico, and a few weeks later, my mother and my brother and his wife, Anne, arrived from Ocean City, New Jersey for a visit, which, as it turned out, was to be my last visit with my mother. She died of congestive heart failure shortly after their return to Ocean City. Peggy and I flew up for the funeral, and she was laid to rest with my father in Arlington National Cemetery.

Mark decided to leave Winston Churchill High School, and joined us in Roosevelt Roads where he enrolled in Roosevelt Roads High School for his senior year. By this time, Mark had become a tall, muscular lad who was a tackle on the state champion football team at Churchill. The coach at Roosevelt Roads was delighted to have him on the team, and Mark also was the track team's shotput and discus man in the spring. Lisa had returned to FSU to take the courses needed to qualify for teaching at the secondary level, so we still had only one of our flock with us. Because Mark could not stay alone, Peggy remained at home during the first two months of UNITAS XVIII.

It was during her stay with us in Puerto Rico that Lisa, while working at the Officers Club, met a young naval flight officer, Lieutenant (Junior Grade) Rick Hunter. Rick was in Puerto Rico with his squadron, VF-11, training for their imminent deployment to the Mediterranean on board the Forrestal.

At dinner one evening, Lisa casually mentioned meeting Rick, and asked if she could invite him for dinner the following evening. The next day, as the time for dinner approached, a car drew up in front of our quarters. Lisa had been working at the club that afternoon, and Peggy and I saw a young, good-looking officer get out of the car, come around to the passenger side, where he opened the door, and out stepped our daughter who until that moment, had refused to let a man open a door for her in the name of female independence. Peggy said, "This looks pretty serious."

When they entered, Lisa introduced us to Rick. As we shook hands, Rick told me that he flew in the F-4's of the World Famous Red Rippers, with a look indicating that he expected me to congratulate him on being part of such a famous squadron. I said, "I am sorry but I never heard of the Red Rippers." When I saw his crest-fallen reaction, I regretted my words, true though they were. However, we soon enjoyed chatting with Rick, and were happy to see how much he and Lisa took to one another. Rick is now a cherished son-in-law.

UNITAS XVIII commenced on 29 July 1977, with the arrival at Roosevelt Roads of the flagship, the USS Mahan (DDG-42), accompanied by the frigates USS Vreeland (FF-1068) and USS Capodanno (FF-1093). The squadron commander, Captain T--- K---, a 1952 classmate, rode in Vreeland. The commanding officer of Mahan was Commander Bob Soupiset, an excellent skipper, well liked by his crew.

On 5 August, our ships set out for Santa Marta, Colombia, to begin a counter-clockwise transit around South America., After a one-day stop at Santa Marta, where we were joined by several frigates of the Colombian Navy, we steamed to Cartagena, Colombia, the major base of the Colombian Navy and the site of their headquarters.

Cartagena is on the Caribbean Sea, and during the days when Spain was reaping hoards of gold and silver from its colonies, Cartagena was the staging point for the fleets of galleons that carried the treasure to Spain. The old city, therefore, is surrounded by massive stone walls intended to thwart the raids of the pirates who swept the Spanish Main in those days of tall ships and rugged sailors. The walls also provided a strong means of defense against would-be invaders, as Admiral Vernon, Royal Navy, learned when he laid siege to Cartagena in 1746. Anticipating victory, Vernon had had coins struck depicting the surrender of the city to him. In the event, Vernon was unsuccessful, with his sailors and the accompanying soldiers being swept by fevers that rendered his force inadequate to the task. The coins were discovered in the mud of the bottom of the harbor, and Capitan de Navio Rafael Grau Araujo, commander of the naval base and an old friend from his attaché days in Washington, gave me three of them, relics that I highly prize.

Since I was unaccompanied by Peggy , my South American naval friends thought it only right that I should be provided an attractive female escort for the receptions and dinners. While I appreciated their thoughtfulness, I kept the escorts at arm's length, something my friends found difficult to understand. By the time we arrived in Chile, the word had reached the Navy people, probably received from their attaches, and there were no more escorts provided.

We proceeded through the Panama Canal, and during the ensuing cruise, we visited Salinas, Ecuador (I was struck by the beauty of the women of Ecuador); Paita, Callao, and Ilo, Peru; Iquique, Mejillones, Puerto Aldea, Valparaiso, Talcahuano, and Punta Arenas, Chile; and arrived at Montevideo, Uruguay on 14 October 1977.

Due to the criticism from Washington of the Junta that had taken control of the government of Argentina, we were not invited to stop in that unfortunate country. It was the Junta that subsequently decided to invade the Falklands, claiming that those remote and wind-swept islands rightly belonged to Argentina. The Junta never thought that far-off Britain would bother, or could bother, to defend the islands, and were shocked when Prime Minister Margaret Thatcher sent a task force of navy ships bearing Royal Marines and Royal Army troops to indeed defend their British subjects.

In the ensuing conflict, the Royal Navy lost several destroyers to attacks from Argentine aircraft, and the Argentine Navy lost the cruiser Belgrano, torpedoed with heavy loss of life. The naval battle could be called a draw, but the Argentine soldier, a draftee in his teens with only rudimentary training, was no match for the Brits on land, and soon the defeat of the Junta was evident. The Falklands remain one of the last vestiges of the mighty British Empire.

As a result of their defeat, the Junta were removed from power, and the good people of Argentina now have a democratic elected government.

As we approached the pier in Montevideo, I was surprised and delighted to see Peggy standing there. As soon as the brow was secured to the quarterdeck, she came aboard, accompanied by the greeting party from the Uruguayan Navy. After a brief exchange of pleasantries with our hosts, they went off with Captain Van Dusen to go over the plans for that evening, while Peggy and I went to my cabin. We were there only a few minutes when Skip Van Dusen knocked on my cabin door, and informed me that the young squadron doctor from the Vreeland was on board and had critical information that I needed to hear immediately. Peggy told me she would wait for me at the hotel where she had booked a room for us, and left.

When the doctor entered, he handed me a green bound book, the type used to keep a record, a log as the Navy terms it. He asked me to read it, which I did. It was a record of the often irrational and erratic behavior of Captain K., a record that clearly indicated that Captain K. was suffering from a mental problem and was unfit to continue as squadron commander. I called for Captain Van Dusen, and had him read it. When he finished, he quietly said, "Shall I send for Captain K.?"

I nodded, and added that he should also alert the crew of the P-3 to be ready to fly to Florida within the next two hours. As I waited for

Skip to return with Captain K., I felt the heavy weight of the action that I felt I must take, especially since he was a classmate.

T. K. entered with a cheery greeting, and asked what it was that I wanted. I glanced at Skip, who shook his head, indicating that he had not told T. K. why I had sent for him. I then told T. K. that I had strong reason to believe that he needed medical help, and that I was relieving him and sending him to Florida for evaluation and treatment. His attitude immediately changed to one of sarcastic defiance, and he said he knew that I had been out to get him ever since we were midshipmen. He added that he had had those evaluations before and those doctors were idiots who were easily fooled, and he would see who got relieved when he got to Florida. Skip reminded him that he was speaking to his superior officer, and again his attitude abruptly changed. He drew up to attention, saluted me and said he was ready to carry out my orders. Skip had told our staff to prepare orders for T.'s flight to Mayport, so I signed the orders, handed them to T., and told him to carry out the orders in hand. He saluted again and left, accompanied by Skip who flew with him all the way.

Skip returned with the P-3 two days later, and informed me that T. had remained silent throughout the flight. However, when Skip started to escort him to his group commander, Rear Admiral C., T. strongly rejected Skip's doing so, and said he was a man of honor so it was not necessary for Skip to escort him as if he was a prisoner. So Skip did not go with T. to RADM C..'s office, and left after watching T. go into the group headquarters building.

Our next port was Rio de Janeiro, where we arrived on 28 October. I had sent CincLantFlt a report immediately after sending T. to Florida, and a letter awaited me in Rio, from the destroyer type commander, a vice admiral, advising me that Rear Admiral C. was bringing charges against me for improper use of authority, inasmuch as I had relieved T. K. without just cause. The type commander, as the convening authority if there was to be a court-martial, was advising me accordingly by letter rather than by message, the letter requiring my signature and return as proof of delivery to me. I kept a copy of the letter, signed the original, and sent it to our naval attaché for delivery to Norfolk. I then sat down and using the log kept by the doctor, recorded in detail in a message to

Admiral Kidd the descriptions of the incidents recorded by the doctor. It took me about four hours to write the message, which then had to be encrypted before sending, which took another four hours. Finally, the message was sent and I calculated that I should be hearing some sort of response from Norfolk the next day. However, it was not until after we arrived at Salvador, Brazil, on 4 November that a message came from Norfolk, advising me that a member of the LantFlt staff would meet us at Trinidad on our arrival on 16 November to conduct an investigation in accordance with the Uniform Code of Military Justice.

It was on Vreeland that the incidents had occurred, so I went over to Vreeland and addressed the entire ship's company, telling them of the impending investigation and exhorting them to stand up and not be afraid to tell the investigating officer all that had occurred during the cruise.

After a stop at Fortaleza, Brazil, we proceeded to Trinidad, arriving on schedule on 16 November. Captain Dick Dallamura was waiting for us, and spent the next two days interviewing members of the Vreeland crew and members of Captain K.'s staff, especially the doctor. We sailed from Trinidad on 18 November, and Captain Dallamura flew back to Norfolk the same day. On 20 November, shortly before our arrival at Puerto La Cruz, Venezuela, a message was received from CincLanfFlt informing me that Captain Dallamura's report substantiated my report, and advising that Rear Admiral C., when given Dallamura's report, withdrew all charges, and requested retirement. Captain T. K. also retired, closing the incident. The type commander sent a back channel to me, thanking me for what I had done, and sent another captain from his staff to take T.'s place.

We completed the operation with stops at La Guaira, Venezuela, and Willemstad, in the Dutch West Indies. Peggy had flown back to Puerto Rico from Rio, since she didn't wish to be away from home and Mark too long. On 3 December, the staff and I boarded the P-3 for the flight home, after first bidding farewell to our ships that also set course for home. Thus ended an unusual UNITAS.

We had expected to have a period of a month or so after the holidays to relax, but other plans for us were afoot.

The day after Christmas, I received a phone call at our quarters from Frank Kelso, Admiral Kidd's executive assistant, informing me that Admiral Kidd wished to speak with me.

"Hello, Jimmy. This is Ike Kidd."

"Yes, sir. How are you?"

"Jimmy, I need to speak to you up here in my office. Can you be up here tomorrow for a 1300 meeting in my office?"

"Yes, sir."

I immediately called the commanding officer of the naval air station at Roosevelt Roads, Captain Bob Rasmussen, and told him of my conversation with Admiral Kidd. Bob said he would call back in ten minutes.

True to his word, Bob called and informed me that he had received permission from Commander, Patrol Wings Atlantic, to use a P-3 to carry me to Norfolk, departing at 0800.

The next day, I arrived at CincLantFlt headquarters at 1245, and was immediately taken in to Admiral Kidd's office.

"Good afternoon, sir!"

"Sit down, Jimmy. I have an important and exciting assignment for ComSoLant. The Soviets have been diligently working on improving relations with the countries of West Africa, no doubt to gain favored access to the petroleum and other resources there, but we think also to get a few naval bases there as well. If they could base their attack submarines at a few select ports on the west coast of Africa, they would have easy access to the sea lines of communications in the Atlantic, similar to the advantage Germany gained with the fall of France in the Second World War. So after considerable discussion among representatives from the White House, State and Defense, and over the strident objections of some at State but with the strong support of others from State, President Carter has ordered the Navy to conduct a 'show-the-flag' operation in West Africa. To do this, you will have the Inchon as your flagship, carrying a company of recon Marines, six CH-46 helos, two of the presidential helos, and the Marine Drum and Bugle Corps. The entire Marine contingent will be commanded by a colonel who will report to you. You will also have the USS Spruance and three other destroyers for escorts."

"You are to make an undetected transit from Norfolk to

Casablanca, Morocco, your first port of call, where you will have to charm the Moroccans without the aid of the ambassador, who is one of those opposed to sending in the Navy. But none in the opposition have come up with an alternate plan other than steaming as before, which is not cutting it. Any questions?"

"Yes, sir. Do the presidential helos mean that President Carter will be going to Africa while we are there?"

Admiral Kidd looked at me with a look that told me I had just asked Dumb Question of the Year.

"No, Jimmy. You are to use those helos to ferry the presidents, or prime ministers, the ministers of defense, and the top military to and from the Inchon."

"Here's the drill. You will pick up the VIPs and carry them to Inchon where the Marines, including the Drum and Bugle Corps, will render honors on the flight deck. Then you will invite them into the wardroom for a steak dinner, after which you then invite them to a 'display of Marine capabilities' at a site selected by our naval attaché, carrying them again in the presidential helos. You will land at the selected site, where some folding chairs will have been set up by the attaché, and ask them to please be seated. In the distance, the sound of helos will be heard, growing ever louder. Then, in a roar of engines and whirling helo blades, the Marines will rapidly rappel down from the hovering helos, and will set up a perimeter defense, all within two minutes of their appearance. Your Marine colonel will narrate what is happening, as it occurs. When the drill is completed, the colonel will call in the presidential helos for the trip back to the designated location where cars will be waiting to take your guests to their offices. I expect there will be a formal reception and dinner presented by the host country. Any other questions?"

"Yes, sir. When will the cruise start and will we be flying over there for the usual planning conferences, as we do for UNITAS?"

"The cruise will start as soon as your ships are assembled here, and the Marines have embarked on Inchon. Obviously, there will be no planning seminars. You will have to work with the attaches to get things set up. After Morocco you will visit Senegal; Liberia; Cote d'Ivoire; Ghana, and last, Gabon."

I returned to Puerto Rico that evening, and found the staff waiting for me, anxious to hear what had transpired in my meeting with Admiral Kidd. They were excited and apprehensive at the same time, when they learned what we were tasked to do. Their apprehension was due to the anticipated reaction of our wives since we had been home less than a month, and now were going to be gone for another three months. I told them to call their wives and ask them to come to headquarters for some important news.

When all of the wives were assembled, including Peggy, I told them what we were going to do, stressing the need to counter the Soviet presence in West Africa, and the compliment it was to their husbands that we had been chosen for the task. There was obvious disappointment shown, but also understanding and acceptance, helped by Peggy's comment that Navy wives could handle this, and would hold down the home front as always.

On Wednesday, 3 January 1978, we flew to Norfolk, having spent the past week working out a *modus operandi* with naval attaches of the countries to be visited, all by classified messages. With the exception of Morocco, we followed the scenario suggested by Admiral Kidd. My chief of staff would fly into the country next on the list, and he and the naval attaché were to select the site, with the consent of the senior military officer of the host country, who was to be fully briefed as to our planned display, with the request that he not divulge anything to his civilian superiors or anyone else. The plan for Morocco was a simple port visit, with a wreath-laying ceremony if they so desired. This arrangement was in deference to the U.S. ambassador's request, he being a vocal opponent of the cruise to West Africa.

We sailed on Thursday, 4 January 1978, under total EMCON, meaning ships and helos could not use any electronic or radio equipment, in order to prevent possible detection of our ships as we steamed across the North Atlantic. We also set course on a rhumb line, rather than taking the usual great circle route, since the Soviets probably stationed their overhead photo satellites to cover the latter. All ship-to-ship communications were by flashing light, with tactical signals done by flag hoists. It was a good drill for the signalmen who worked far more than usual, something that they seemed to enjoy, especially since they now were the sole means of communicating.

The day before our arrival at Casablanca, I flew by helo to each ship, where I told the crews of the importance of our mission, and the need for each of them to be an ambassador of the United States, with no bad behavior by anyone. It must have had an impact, because there were no incidents of any kind during the entire cruise.

We were less than a hundred miles from Casablanca when we encountered a group of Soviet fishing vessels, one of whom detached from the group and began following us. Norfolk later informed us by message that the discovery of our task group had caused considerable stir in Moscow, especially at the naval headquarters. The Soviet trawler followed us right into the port of Casablanca, no doubt radioing a detailed description of our ships.

The US ambassador chose to remain in Rabat rather than join a group of his country's naval ships. He defended this action on the grounds of poor health, and sent a junior foreign service officer to meet us and to act as my interpreter since I spoke no French. The Moroccan Navy was delighted to have us there, we being the first U.S. Navy ships to visit since the 1940's, or so we were told.

They provided a car and driver as well as a captain who escorted us. The day after our arrival, the captain came aboard in casual civilian attire, and asked me if I would like to visit Marrakesh, an invitation I readily accepted.

It was a trip into the Arabian Nights. After crossing miles and miles of nothing but desolate desert, there arose out of the distance the towers of the walled city, dramatically highlighted by the late morning sun. We first had some refreshments, fruit and cool drinks of a sweet juice mixture. Then we walked into the old walled part of the city where we entered the huge casbah, the market place covered by canvas that went on for several hundred yards. At the entrance to the casbah was a man garbed in a turban, knee length knickers, a vest of many colorful beads, and carrying a brass water dispenser from which he sold water in a brass cup used by all whose thirst it satisfied.

The casbah was a labyrinth of stalls and tables, with the wares loudly proclaimed by their attendants, describing the great value to be had by purchasing their products. A large section was devoted to the sale and display of the black carbon used to line the eyes of women, the rest of their faces being veiled. Beaten brassware also occupied a good bit of the market. Meat was bought on the hoof, with the lamb or goat then slaughtered and butchered. Clothing, furniture, chess sets, carved ivory figures, and various other such items were in abundance. The section where food was sold was the last visited by us, where we bought shish kebob cooked over charcoal as we waited.

Several hours passed in walking through the casbah, and several could have been added, but our escort advised that we needed to reach Casablanca before sundown, so we left the casbah and headed back out into the desert for the return trip. The sun now was to the west, and shimmering mirages played before our eyes, looking like glistening water in the distance.

The next morning, just as I was finishing breakfast in the wardroom, the young captain who was our escort came aboard, and excitedly informed me that the prime minister was arriving and had asked to meet with me at 1030. I was told that the entourage would arrive at the ship at 1000 to take me to the meeting. My interpreter was present when this transpired, and made a hurried exit to the telephone in order to inform the ambassador in Rabat.

At 1000 sharp, three black sedans with flags fluttering from the fenders pulled up, and off we went. After a short ride across the city, we arrived at a building where an honor guard of spahis mounted on camels were in formation, as well as trumpeters who lined an upper balcony that ran the length of the building. With a wonderful blast from the trumpets, I reviewed the honor guard, and then was directed into the interior courtyard, in the center of which was a large fountain. The entire sides of the walls were covered with blue tiles of the size used in mosaics, the effect of which in the sunlight was indeed dramatic.

As we entered the inner court, we were met by the prime minister, a young man who I gathered was a member of the royal family. We began chatting, I using the interpreter. In the course of the chat, the prime minister asked what I had been doing prior to our visit to Morocco, and I explained that we had been engaged in a trip around South America, exercising with the navies of the countries of South America. In Spanish, he asked if I spoke Spanish, and when I replied that I did, in Spanish, of course, he switched to Spanish, and my poor State escort/interpreter was left guessing as to what was said. I don't know how he handled that in his report to the ambassador. In any event, the prime minister said that the King was glad to have us visiting Morocco, and that it was the King who had told the prime minister to personally convey his welcome, hence the meeting, all of which I dutifully reported to Norfolk, with copy to the ambassador.

The next port of call was Dakar, Senegal. Senegal was formerly a colony of France, and French influence was still very evident. The Senegalese armed forces consisted of a well-trained army, a small air force, and a coast guard. Senegalese troops had fought in both world wars as part of the French Army and had earned a reputation as fierce fighters, especially in the First World War. We were thus hosted by the chief of staff of the army.

The evening of our arrival, an informal reception was held in the large garden next to the headquarters. Several large open fires were burning, over each of which were whole lambs slowly rotating on spits. The fragrance of roasted lamb filled the warm evening air. I was chatting with the chief of staff, with both of us using a patois of French, Spanish and English to converse, a method that was working surprisingly well. About a half hour into the reception, the general's aide informed him that the lamb reserved for us was ready to be eaten. The general walked over to the roasted lamb, still on the spit, and deftly extracted the eyeballs with a long fork, placing them on a small plate. He turned to me and smilingly offered the plate to me, the eyeballs being a prized delicacy, but not by me. I took the plate, thanked the general, and then said it would give me great pleasure to have the general enjoy the offered delicacy. Without any hesitation, he said, "Merci," scooped the eyeballs off the plate and popped them into his mouth, with obvious pleasure. We then each were handed a large plate and a sharp knife, and following the general's lead, I carved off some lamb which I found to be delicious.

The next morning, we were given a tour of the armed forces facilities, including their airbase, where I observed a company of French paratroopers loading onto a transport aircraft, together with a company of Senegalese paratroopers. The French were accompanied by a colonel who came over to our group and asked the Senegalese officer with us who we were and why were we there. After being told we were American naval officers whose ships were in port for an official visit, he came over to me, saluted, and chatted for a few minutes in English, then excused himself and boarded the plane. Our escort informed me that the colonel was the French military attaché, and said that he was active in promoting the combined exercises with the French.

I returned to the ship, and shifted into dress blues, in preparation for the first of what would be standard receptions of dignitaries aboard the Inchon. As arranged by our naval attaché, the two presidential helos had flown into the headquarters helo pad where they embarked the minister of defense, the chief of staff, and several of their senior staff members. On Inchon, the Marine honor guard and the Marine Corps Drum and Bugle Corps were in formation on the flight deck, where I joined them while waiting for the helos to arrive. Soon the familiar sound of helos approaching was heard. I welcomed the visitors as they descended from the aircraft, which then taxied to the other end of the flight deck. The drum corps struck up the anthem of Senegal, followed by "The Stars and Stripes Forever," as we trooped the line. The Marines then passed in review, showing the smartness and precision that are a hallmark of the Marines.

In the wardroom, we sat down to a dinner of tenderloin and potatoes, followed by a dessert of ice cream fudge sundaes. Our guests appeared to be enjoying the dinner, at the end of which, I rose and gave a short speech in which I expressed our friendship for the people of Senegal, and our wish for continued good relations. The minister of defense responded in similar fashion.

I took them on a brief tour of Inchon, and then invited them to board the helos that were on deck with rotors turning. We lifted off and headed in toward the north of the city. I told the minister of defense that we had one more item for him and his party to see.

While we had been having dinner, the Marine CH-46 squadron had taken a company of recon Marines to the site where we were now headed, and had practiced for the display that the Senegalese party were about to see. Only the chief of staff knew what was coming, and it was evident that he was eagerly looking forward to it.

We landed in an open field in which were a group of folding chairs. I invited the minister and his party to be seated, and no sooner had they done so when the faint blip-blip sound of helos could be heard, rapidly growing louder and louder. Then, suddenly, the helos, in tight formation, rose into view. Abruptly stopping in a hover above the field, the helos simultaneously paid out lines down which Marines rapidly rapelled to the ground. In less than two minutes, the Marines had set up a perimeter defense with machine guns and rifles. The Senegalese were suitably impressed, and congratulated the young Marine lieutenant colonel when he approached, saluted, and reported that the area was secure. We re-embarked in the waiting presidential helos for the ride to their headquarters. After landing, the minister of defense invited me to his office, where we sipped very strong coffee from demitasse cups. The minister was effusive in his praise of the Marines, and in expressing his gratitude for our visit. He commented that he and his colleagues had been increasingly concerned about the growing Soviet presence in West Africa, and he was now much relieved because of our presence.

The American ambassador was present for all of the proceedings, and was strongly supportive. That evening, he held a reception in our honor at his quarters, with dinner, dancing, and a swim in his large pool. He expressed his hope that the U.S. Navy would make such visits more frequently, once a year at the least.

It was two down, and four to go, and we were now three weeks into our deployment. After a short cruise along the coast, we steamed into Monrovia, Liberia. This was a country with a unique history.

In the second quarter of the nineteenth century, a group of Americans from the South primarily, concerned about the impact of slavery on Southern society, formed an organization dedicated to buying slaves and transporting them to Africa to begin life anew as free people. The result was the founding of the country that was named Liberia, denoting their freedom from slavery, and the town of Monrovia was established, named in honor of President James Monroe. The country was organized by counties that were named for Southern states, Virginia, Maryland , etc. The former slaves, having lived in America, were more knowledgeable than the indigenous tribes, and thus became the aristocracy of Liberia, an irony of history. There was a large gap between the standard of living enjoyed by the descendants of the founders and the much lower level experienced by the indigenous people.

I was met by the naval chief of staff, a captain, who escorted me to the president's headquarters, a tower-like structure that rose some hundred feet above the main plaza of the town. At the door, I was surrounded by a group of five young men, very well dressed in business suits, with the small earphones used by our Secret Service. Not a word was spoken as we rode up to the top in our well-guarded elevator. I was met by the President, Tubman by name, I think. He was a portly man with silver-gray hair, and was wearing a gray Nehru suit. He took me out onto the balcony that overlooked the small plaza, where a crowd had gathered. Using a microphone, he explained who we were, stressed the importance of our visit, and expressed the hope that we would soon return.

That evening, we were treated to a dinner in our honor, consisting of chitlings and greens, which in the Liberian memory was the food eaten by Americans. Prior to our arrival, we had received an intelligence report that identified the KGB head as a reporter from TASS, the Russian news agency. As we were walking down the path to the entrance of the building where the dinner was being held, we passed through a line of reporters and photographers. The intelligence report had included a recent photo of the KGB agent, and I spotted him among the reporters. On impulse, I strode over to him, shook his hand, and exclaimed, "Tovarish, nastdrovya!" His startled face went pale, and he gave me a weak smile. The next day, he was on his way back to Russia, and the American intelligence folks were most unhappy with me because now they did not know who was the KGB man in Monrovia. Their displeasure was fully understood by me. It was a dumb thing to do.

The year after we visited Liberia, a Sergeant Doe of the Liberian Army led a coup to overthrow the government, during which the president was taken down to the beach where he was flailed alive, with salt water poured over his bleeding body, and was then doused with gasoline and burned .

We continued on down the west coast of Africa, with our next country to visit being Cote D'Ivoire, the Ivory Coast. This was followed by Ghana, and finally, the last country, Gabon. At each country, the same routine was followed, with similar results. Our presence provided a strong counter to the inroads being attempted by the Soviet Union, and overall the cruise was successful in attaining its objective. I was extremely pleased with the conduct of all hands who participated, with not a single incident occurring in any country visited.

The visit to Gabon brought the ships to the equator, so those polliwogs on board were duly initiated into the realm of King Neptune, thus acquiring the coveted status of shellbacks. On the Mahan, the traditional rebellion of the polliwogs occurred on the eve of the day we crossed the equator, and I was taken prisoner by three masked polliwogs who took me to a storeroom and left me there, locking the door as they departed. A cot had been placed in the room so I could sleep while being held captive. After a while, I noticed a ship's telephone on a small table in the corner. On the phone, someone had placed a list of phone numbers, one of which was the bridge. I dialed the bridge number, and was greeted by the Officer of the Deck. I informed him of my situation and told him I wished to stay where I was, but could he find out, who would have a key to the space where I was. Several minutes later, he called with the information, and verified that the individual was a polliwog.

At 0600, I was awakened by the entrance of a polliwog, still masked, announcing that I was free to go. Later, when the initiation commenced, I had the culprits brought before me, and I congratulated them for their derring-do, and informed them that they had earned the admiration of the shellbacks, and so they would be getting special attention as they proceeded through the initiation. They "enjoyed" extra trips through the slop chute and the gauntlet, but it was all in good form and all hands had fun as they should have.

The force returned to Norfolk, where it disbanded. I made my report to Admiral Kidd, and the staff and I flew to Roosevelt Roads and home. This cruise to West Africa was the first of a continuing series of visits by the Navy to those waters.

In May, 1978, I received a phone call from a captain in BuPers, informing me that I was to fly to Washington the following week for an interview with the under secretary of the Navy, James Woolsey, having been nominated by the Chief of Naval Operations for the directorship of the Office of Program Appraisal in the Office of the secretary of the Navy.

18

Back to the Pentagon

Having been approved by Mr. Woolsey, with the concurrence of the secretary of the Navy, Graham Claytor, I was relieved of my ComSoLant duties by Rear Admiral J. J. Ekelund, class of 1949 and also a submariner, on 23 June 1978, and reported for duty as Director, Office of Program Appraisal, on 21 July. After spending a week of turn-over and indoctrination, I relieved Ron Hays, a naval aviator, class of 1950, who donned a third star as Deputy CincLantFlt in Norfolk, VA.

Admiral Kidd had retired from the Navy shortly after my departure from the ComSoLant billet, and although his last fitness report for me stated that I was decorated on detachment, no such medal was received, probably due to his departure from active duty, allowing the making of such an award to drop through the cracks, as the saying goes. I chose not to pursue the matter, since doing so would have caused Admiral Kidd some embarrassment.

The Office of Program Appraisal occupied a unique position within the Navy headquarters organization. A staff office of the secretary of the Navy, its mission was "to assist the secretary in assuring that existing and proposed Navy and Marine Corps programs provide(d) the optimum means of achieving the objectives of the Department of the Navy." This was achieved by analysis of objectives and determining the validity, adequacy, feasibility and balance of proposed programs to meet them; monitoring Department studies to keep the secretary informed of their progress, and of problem areas encountered;

appraising all Navy and Marine Corps programs , program change requests, program change decisions, and other procedural documents used in the Defense programming system, as well as SecDef Draft Presidential Memoranda and the secretary's responses to them; conducting any special studies requested by the secretary; and preparing the secretary's Annual Posture Statement to the Congress, the annual report to the President on the work, expenditures, and accomplishments of the Department of the Navy, major speeches given by the secretary, and numerous analyses of force level and weapon system requirements.

In general, therefore, OPA served as a primary consultant to the secretary of the Navy in developing and supporting Department of the Navy positions on force levels, weapon systems, and major programs. Thus, it was necessary to maintain close liaison with the three and four star offices where the programs were initiated, especially the three warfare "barons," the Deputy CNO's for Surface Warfare, Submarine Warfare, and Air Warfare, respectively. It was not uncommon for OPA analysis to differ with the rationale of a program initiating office, requiring diplomatic discussions between OPA and the pertinent office, with the three star himself often directly involved. Maintaining objectivity and a detached view of programs were both *sine qua non*, requiring that my small staff and I had to resist the pressures of our friends and our particular warfare branches. As might be expected, we were not always successful in avoiding the wrath of an office whose proposed program had been disapproved by the secretary. But most understood our role and accepted that we had to do our work in a neutral and objective way.

The first year in OPA passed quickly, it seemed, and I found Secretary Claytor to be an excellent man to work for, with a quick grasp of issues, an open mind, and a good knowledge of the working Navy dating from his service in the navy in World War II when he commanded a destroyer escort. In June of 1979, he was moved up to the Deputy Secretary of Defense job, the number two man in the Defense Department. His good friend, Edward Hidalgo, who had been the Assistant Secretary of the Navy for Research and Development, was moved up to the Secretary position, causing the departure of

Jim Woolsey, the Deputy Secretary under Claytor, with that position being filled by Mr. Murray, whose style was much different from Woolsey's. Murray was a detail man, that is, he got into minutiae that Woolsey had left to the lower echelons to handle, causing the detail work in OPA to increase proportionately, with no apparent increase in efficiency or production within the office of the Secretary of the Navy. Mr. Hidalgo had been an air intelligence officer during the war, and had little knowledge of the Navy as a whole, despite having had several years as ASN for R & D. Thus, the great bulk of work within the secretariat was left to Mr. Murray, who diligently pursued his tasks. However, this arrangement caused a loss of confidence in Mr. Hidalgo throughout the headquarters among both civilians and uniformed personnel, with a consequent loss of cooperation of the several offices within the headquarters with our people in OPA. Previously, our requests for information were quickly met, but under Mr. Hidalgo's regime, we found increasing resistance, causing our work to become much more difficult. All on my staff, both civilians and naval officers, bore down and put in the extra hours needed to meet our tasks, a result of the outstanding leadership of my deputies, first Captain Jack Baldwin, and his successor, Captain Zap Zlatoper. Both later attained senior flag rank.

Secretaries Claytor and Hidalgo served in the administration of President Carter, and with the arrival of newly elected President Reagan, substantial changes among the civilian appointees necessarily occurred, chief of which was the arrival of John Lehman as the new Secretary of the Navy.

Thirty-eight years of age, Mr. Lehman was the youngest individual to be appointed Secretary of the Navy. Ebullient and self-confident to the point of brashness, young Lehman tended to be less than diplomatic in his dealings with the flag officers who were all years his senior in age. I found myself in the middle of a growing wave of resentment among the three and four stars who inhabited the E Ring of the Navy section of the Pentagon. I was identified as being a part of Secretary Lehman's coterie, and was thus subject to the same criticism as was being directed at Mr. Lehman. Among my two-star peers within the Pentagon, I tried to persuade them of the positive changes

I saw being made within the Secretariat, all of which Mr. Lehman instituted for the good of the Navy. Only his selection for the post of ASN (R&D) did I find detrimental to the Navy.

I was particularly excited about the initiative to bring the Navy back up to the strength seen as needed in order to counter effectively the world-wide probes of the Soviet Navy, an initiative that became known as "The 600 Ship Navy." It was Mr. Lehman who had persuaded President Reagan of the need to build up to that level and it was he who was tirelessly campaigning for support from the Congress in the form of increased appropriations for the Navy's shipbuilding account, labeled SCN in the parlance of the Pentagon. He may have been more effective if he had taken a lower-keyed approach with Congress, but by the end of President Reagan's second term, the Navy numbered just under 600 ships, thanks to John Lehman, a level never again attained so far (2015). In fact, as of 2015, the Navy has less than 280 ships, and continues to decline in numbers because not enough ships are being built to equal the number reaching the age to be retired, which is 30 years for most classes of naval vessels.

In positive things accomplished for the Navy during his tenure as secretary of the Navy, John Lehman strongly resembled another naval enthusiast who was Assistant Secretary of the Navy, and later was president, a man greatly admired by John Lehman. I am speaking of Theodore Roosevelt. John Lehman was a truly exceptional civilian leader of the Navy.

By June of 1981, I had been Director of OPA for three years, had served three different secretaries, and considering that I was now on the wrong side of a number of the "barons" in Navy headquarters, I decided to retire at the end of September, and so informed Mr. Lehman by a personal memo to him. About an hour after I had sent my memo to his office, Mr. Lehman strode in to my office with my memo in hand and informed me that he would not approve of my retiring. Instead, he told me that the Assistant Secretary of Defense for International Security Affairs, Mr. Francis "Bing" West, had requested that I be assigned to him as a special assistant, and he asked me to withdraw my memo, which I reluctantly did.

Several weeks later, my classmate, C. C. Smith, arrived to relieve me, and I then reported to Secretary West for duty. C. C. and I had been in the same company at the Academy, and he had been the company commander our first-class year. Secretary Lehman was a naval aviator in the Naval Reserve, and had requested a naval aviator as my relief, thus, C.C. was selected, he being a fighter pilot who had commanded USS Enterprise, the Navy's first nuclear-powered carrier.

I was with Mr. West only a few months, but in that time I worked on a briefing for the prime minister and minister of defense for Israel, which I then presented to the Israelis, all of whom were very courteous except for the minister of defense, who was clearly opposed to the project being briefed. The issue was still being discussed when I left, so I never knew the outcome.

I also represented Mr. West in discussions with House and Senate staffers on a project in Honduras, which was approved by the Congress.

The Pentagon maintains a list of flag officers who are willing to make speeches to civic associations, veterans organizations, etc., when such groups request a speaker. I made two trips to give speeches, one to the Midwest and one to Boston. The former was an address to the Kiwanis Club of the Tri-Cities area, held at a hotel in Moline, Illinois, and included an interview on the local radio as well as one on local television. With these plus the speech, I was engaged as a Defense spokesman the entire day. The occasion was the observance of Pearl Harbor Day, and I felt honored to be the Defense representative for that occasion. The subject of my speech was "Silent Heroes," a topic dealing with the many unseen acts of heroism that occur in combat, such as covering your platoon or ship mates, caring for any wounded in your immediate area, and doing the many things, small in nature, but important for survival and for overcoming the enemy.

I enjoyed the opportunity to meet civilians and explain the whats and whys of events occurring in Washington and wherever our armed forces were located.

In mid- December of 1981, I was called to Secretary Lehman's office, where he informed me that I was to be interviewed the next day by Mrs. Anne Armstrong, who was the newly appointed chairman of the President's Foreign Intelligence Advisory Board.

The PFIAB, pronounced "Piffiab," had been disestablished by President Carter, and was now being reestablished by President Reagan. It was first established by President Kennedy who disputed the analysis of the CIA regarding the level of Soviet achievement in developing and fielding inter-continental missiles capable of delivering nuclear warheads against targets in the United States. Kennedy wanted an independent assessment to be done, and appointed a group of military and civilians who were a mix of business men and persons trained in intelligence. As a result of the PFIAB's findings, the United States embarked upon a major effort to develop and emplace ICBM's, which eventually were installed in large concrete cylinders built into the ground, known as missile silos, controlled and manned by U.S. Air Force personnel. The Air Force also built a fleet of long range bombers, the B-47, which was later replaced by the B-52, and with the permission of the president and the Congress, General Curtis LeMay, the USAF chief of staff, set up the Strategic Air Command, headed by a four-star Air Force general, headquartered at Omaha, Nebraska.

The Navy carrier aviation community tried to enter the strategic effort, but met with limited success, being out-matched by the Air Force capability for long range bombing. The CNO, Admiral Arleigh Burke, was known for his ability to overcome adversity, and with the assistance of two brilliant men, Rear Admirals Rickover and Raborn, persuaded President Kennedy to approve the development of sea-launched ballistic missiles, to be carried by dedicated submarines each housing sixteen large missile tubes. Quiet submarines with nuclear powered propulsion could remain on station undetected, thus giving the U.S. a survivable leg of the nuclear triad, which ensured our ability to make a return or second strike if attacked by a nation having a ballistic missile capability. It was the accelerated production of the ballistic missile submarine that had led to my being drafted into nuclear power training and into submarines.

Over the years, the PFIAB had become a means for the president to award big supporters by appointing them to the PFIAB, which still necessarily retained a core group of intelligence analysts, plus a professional military officer with training and experience in intelligence who acted as executive director. It was this post that I was being interviewed for, having been recommended by Mr. Lehman when asked to provide an officer for the executive director billet.

The next afternoon, I went to the Old Executive Office Building in which Anne Armstrong and the PFIAB offices were located. Built in the late nineteenth century, the Old Executive Office Building is just west of the White House, and is considered a part of the White House, holding as it does the office of the vice president, as well as other high level offices within the Executive branch of government. Its architecture is unique, being more in the style of an over-size Italian villa. The interior contains several ornate meeting rooms as well as some offices that at one time or another saw some serious history in the making. In 1941, for example, it housed the State Department and the War Department, the latter being the domain of the Secretary of War, there being no Defense Department at that time. The Navy Department had its own building on Constitution Avenue.

It was in one of those offices that the Secretary of State, Cordell Hull, met with the Japanese ambassador who had come to try to persuade the United States to lift the embargoes of oil and other materials needed by Japan for its war against China, the latter war being the reason the embargoes were enacted. The date was 7 December 1941, and it was while the diplomats were talking that the Japanese fleet of carriers struck Pearl Harbor, bringing the United States into the war then being fought in Europe and China, the Second World War.

Working with the PFIAB entailed having a close relationship with the senior officials at the Central Intelligence Agency and the Defense Intelligence Agency. Bob Inman was now a four star admiral, and was the Deputy Director of the CIA, a circumstance that very much benefited my efforts to get the PFIAB back into operation. Anne Armstrong had been the ambassador to the United Kingdom, during which she gained a good knowledge of the workings of the national intelligence establishment.

The Deputy Chairman, Leo Cherne, was a well-known sculptor from New York City, who had gained national prominence with his busts of Washington and Lincoln, copies of which he had donated to the PFIAB. A Democrat, he had served on a previous PFIAB in the Johnson administration. It puzzled me as to why a sculptor should be involved in intelligence, a question that was never resolved.

Other knowledgeable members included two professors from Stanford who had extensive experience with the CIA, and Clare Booth Luce, whose involvement stemmed from her marriage to the long-time publisher of Time magazine. Mrs. Luce was very active with the PFIAB, whereas other members such as Bob Six, founder and CEO of Continental Airlines, enjoyed the quarterly meetings but really had no major contribution to make.

A unique member was Ross Perot, US Naval Academy Class of 1953, with whom I had worked on the implementation of the Honor Concept when we were midshipmen. Ross was and is deeply involved in the POW/MIA issue, trying to resolve the status of those missing in action, those who were known to be POWs but never returned, and caring for the families of those MIAs still unaccounted for.

Immediately upon completion of his obligated service, Ross had resigned from the Navy and went with IBM. Ross saw an opportunity for IBM to expand into the field of data recording, but the executives at IBM would not agree to do so. Ross therefore left IBM and started his own company, which was so successful that Ross now is a billionaire. He has used his wealth for a number of gifts to the Naval Academy, including the statue of Vice Admiral Jim Stockdale, who received the Medal of Honor for his heroic leadership and strong resistance toward his captors during his years as a prisoner of war in North Vietnam. Ross also contributed a statue of Vice Admiral Bill Lawrence, who received the Silver Star for his heroic actions, also while a prisoner of war in North Vietnam.

Ross came to the first meeting of the PFIAB, filled with hope of finally getting information about at least some of the MIAs, but his hopes were not to be realized. When I was working in the office of the Assistant Secretary of Defense (International Security Affairs), I had tried to garner information about my close friend and classmate, Colonel John F. O'Grady, USAF, who had been shot down by a missile while flying a mission in Vietnam. Jack was seen to eject from his crippled aircraft, with parachute fully deployed, and appeared to land safely on the ground. His wingman had to depart before the rescue helo arrived, and when the latter arrived, some twenty minutes after the wingman had departed, there was no sign of O'Grady, who never was seen again by Western eyes. To my chagrin, I was told that I was off limits with my query, and was further told to drop it. Thus, when Ross asked me to place discussion of the MIAs on the agenda with the objective of activating the intelligence community to work on finding the MIAs, I told Ross that I did not think it would be possible to do so, but I would raise the subject with Anne Armstrong. Anne passed it on up to Vice President Bush, who said it could not be approved.

Ross was furious. He came to my office and stated if the PFIAB could not get into the MIA area, how could they operate effectively with the intelligence agencies, since their work necessarily got into highly classified information. I told Ross of my experience with the subject at the Pentagon, and was informed by him that if that was so, he was no longer a member of the PFIAB. That was the last meeting of Ross Perot with the PFIAB.

The PFIAB took up several front burner intelligence issues, but it was make-work in my opinion. We did brief President Reagan several times, and were very cordially received by the president. I was surprised by his height, and even more so by his acumen and ready grasp of the issues. The news accounts of Reagan at meetings had him falling asleep and being a very slender reed when it came to intelligence, but he clearly was on top of the issues and asked intelligent questions and made insightful comments.

Being assigned to the White House was more than most of the young staff members I encountered could handle without becoming intoxicated with their proximity to the seat of power, and too many of them ended up acting as if he or she were the president. Having to deal with them was not to my liking, to say the least. Furthermore, I felt that the aura of the White House caused too many of the staff to lose touch with the real world. All of the foregoing made me feel an urgent need to get back with the Navy, and the ten months I spent with the PFIAB was not my favorite tour of duty. I am sure that Anne Armstrong was disappointed with my desire to depart, and I understand her reasons for feeling that way, since it obviously seemed that I was not really interested in doing my duties as executive director. I regret that I may have left her with such an impression, because I very much wanted to see the PFIAB become a viable intelligence aid for the president, and worked to make it so while I was there. However, I could not conceal my delight when my orders arrived, calling me back to the Pentagon for a few months as assistant to the CNO for strategic planning, followed by orders to be the Chief of Naval Education and Training.

The latter orders followed a meeting with Secretary Lehman at which Admiral Jim Watkins, the CNO, was also present, in which Lehman told me that I had a choice to make, either go to the Deputy CinCPacFleet job at Pearl Harbor, or to the position of Chief of Naval Education and Training. He then at some length explained why he was not going to send me to a numbered fleet command, since my major command as a captain had been a shore command, and I thus lacked the fleet experience needed by a fleet commander. I did not mentally agree with that assessment, but I chose not to argue about it. It seemed clear to me that he and the CNO wanted me to take the CNET billet, but had offered the Deputy CinC billet as a gesture of good will or kindness, or something. So I opted for the CNET job. I do not consider myself to be an intellectual, bookish, professorial type, but for reasons that escape me, many others do. I think that same perception influenced Lehman and Watkins to select me for CNET. At any rate, I was being moved up to a vice admiral billet, and I was leaving the Pentagon and Washington, so I was happy to be going down to Pensacola, Florida, where CNET headquarters were located.

19

Pensacola, Florida

Shortly after receiving orders to the CNET billet, I was called to the CNO's office, where Admiral Watkins spent some time describing the problems within the Naval Education and Training Command. He was especially critical of the civilian long-timers who had gone to Pensacola from the Pers-C section of the Bureau of Naval Personnel when the training command was set up in the early 1970s. Pers-C had been the nexus of training in the Navy, and the attitude of too many, in Admiral Watkins' opinion, was that they were the only people who knew how to run the command, leaving little latitude for initiatives outside of the CNET headquarters. The CNET billet had been down-graded to rear admiral prior to Watkins' tour as CNO, and the incumbent, Rear Admiral Ken Shugart, was virtually powerless in dealing with the three star warfare sponsors in Washington. When the Command was established, the decision was made to have CNET's funding be provided by those getting the training, namely, the respective Deputy CNO for Surface Warfare, for Submarine Warfare, and for Air Warfare. After receiving the training requirements for the coming fiscal year, CNET was tasked with providing the sponsors with the respective costs, allocated among the several budget categories such as personnel, operations and maintenance, and construction. It was then up to the sponsor to meet the bill, and as often as not, monies sent to CNET did not cover adequately the costs for operations and maintenance; too often, the sponsors' staffs would make their own judgments as to the need for maintenance, based on how much they needed for the sponsors' priority projects, which often exceeded the amount in their budget. When such a shortage was forecast, the staff would reduce the monies to CNET to cover their own projects, but without reducing their training requirements. So in order to meet the training costs, maintenance funds would be cut. As one might expect, the result was a lot of leaking roofs, barracks in poor condition, and base upkeep generally lacking, all of which had a major impact on morale of both the trainers and the students. Admiral Watkins succeeded in persuading Mr. Lehman that CNET had to be a vice admiral in order to get the command in shape and to keep it so. My work was clearly cut out for me.

As a first step, Admiral Watkins told me to get my additional stripe on my blues, and fly down to Pensacola and then to the outlying commands under CNET, to get a first-hand view of conditions. They were not good, in fact, they were generally worse than I had been led to expect.

The naval air station at Pensacola was rightly named "The Cradle of Naval Aviation," having been the site where Captain Mustin and his fledgling fliers set up training for naval aviators in the early 20th century. But the pride inherent in that label was not reflected in the appearance of the base. Paint was peeling from a number of buildings, landscaping was non-existent, and the general effect was one of disregard for the physical appearance of this historic air station.

Visits to the other bases that were part of the naval air training command found barracks in poor condition, heads with many of the urinals and toilets inoperable, leaking roofs, and over-crowded conditions in the barracks due to the excessive number of officers in the training pipeline for aviators.

The recruit training centers at Great Lakes, Orlando, and San Diego, were in similar condition. Only the submarine training center at Groton, Connecticut, was properly maintained.

I relieved Admiral Shugart on 13 January, 1983, and began compiling data to support going to Washington for a meeting with the surface and air warfare sponsors. I briefed Admiral Watkins the day before the meeting, and when he realized the magnitude of the problem, he ordered a session of the CNO Executive Board to be held in two weeks, and ordered cancellation of the meeting with the two sponsors. Thus, the entire Washington leadership would see the derelict conditions existing, to the embarrassment of the two sponsors involved.

I came to the CEB armed with photos and graphs depicting the problem, and when the dust cleared, both sponsors were told to meet their fiscal requirements in order to get the necessary repairs completed within the next nine months. In the event, the surface warfare sponsor fully met his obligation, but the air warfare sponsor offered less than half of what was needed, opining that conditions were not as bad as I had said.

After I explained to Admiral Watkins how over-crowded the aviation training pipeline was, he approved my taking funds from the pipeline to meet the maintenance requirements. This caused a bit of an uproar among the Washington air staff, but the CNO held firm and the necessary repairs were made. At the same time, morale among the air students and the training squadrons went up, and training moved apace. Rear Admiral Pete Booth was in command of the air training command, and Pete had stood solidly behind my efforts, to the detriment of his standing with the air warfare sponsor. It took courage and strength of character to do that, and Pete possessed both in abundance.

The Naval Reserve Officer Training Corps was one of the many commands under the CNET hat, and it also needed some maintenance. I had served with some of the captains who were now heads of the naval science departments at their respective universities, and they quickly informed me that closer personal attention from CNET would be in order, so the deputy, Rear Admiral Skip Furlong, and I embarked on a program of each of us visiting a different unit each month during the academic year, a program that thus called for 18 universities a year to be visited. Since there were 52 units, all units could be visited over a three-year span. It was an interesting experience, meeting with presidents or chancellors of the various universities involved, noting the differences from one to another. With some, it was money, with others it was a desire to serve the country, and with a few others, it was a reluctant effort pressed upon them by the alumni. In any event, the program was successful in improving the spirit of the units. The outstanding quality and dedication of the officers at the units was a major factor in keeping the program at the high standards needed to produce good officers.

As I recall, it was in the spring of 1985 that Assistant Secretary Paisley persuaded Secretary Lehman that the CNET organization should be abolished. The Naval Material Command had already been disestablished, and now it apparently was CNET's turn. Why Paisley wanted to do so was never revealed to me.

When I was informed of the matter by the Chief of Naval Personnel, I called CNO's executive assistant, Captain Mike Boorda, who told me that CNO was unable to dissuade Mr. Lehman, and that it seemed to be a "done deal." I then called the executive assistant to Mr. Lehman, and learned that Lehman was flying down to Pensacola in a few days, presumably to inform me of his decision.

It was a Friday when the Secretary of the Navy landed at the naval air station, where Skip Furlong and I met him. We escorted him into the Admin Building of the air station, took him into a separate room, shut the door, and then, as forcefully as proper respect would permit, we both bluntly told him that he was making a grievous error, and that shutting down the Navy's training command was simply a dumb idea, particularly when no rationale had been presented for doing so. The Congressman for the Pensacola district was ready to make a federal case out of it, and had told me that if we could not persuade Mr.Lehman to change his mind, the Republican party in the area would get all the blame for the loss of the command and the resulting loss of employment. All of this we forcefully presented to Mr. Lehman, who was quietly listening. Finally, he stood up and raised his hand, saying that there would be no disestablishment of CNET, and that I should inform the staff as soon as possible.

Skip Furlong notified all the staff to assemble in the auditorium, and the tension among them was palpable. I walked up to the dais, and told them that Admiral Furlong and I had just come from a meeting with Secretary Lehman, and that Mr. Lehman had asked us to inform the staff that CNET was staying alive. At first there was a dead silence while the news sank in, then the staff as one broke into a loud cheer, a truly electric moment. It was around 2:30 pm when this happened, and I then told them the staff was dismissed for the weekend, so the celebration could begin. Clearly, no more work was going to be done that afternoon, and the staff happily streamed out of the auditorium.

After calling CNO and BuPers with the news, I then called our Congressman and informed him, to his joyous surprise. My final call was to the editor of the local newspaper, who ran a special edition that afternoon, headlining the news. Skip and I went over to the club and raised a glass in salute to Secretary Lehman, who, by that time, was downtown at his favorite Pensacola spot, Trader John's.

It was one of our better days at CNET.

When I first arrived at CNET headquarters, I was surprised by the size of the staff, which numbered over 400 civilians and some fifty naval personnel. I soon learned that CNO's perception of the staff was correct; the command was being micro-managed by the old Pers-C group, and they had gradually justified growing the staff to its present size. It was no coincidence that numbers being managed by an individual was a basic rationale for that individual's GS level, and showing a wide span of responsibility also helped.

I began the practice of meeting monthly with the immediate subordinate commanders, all of whom were rear admirals and included the two Fleet Training Commands, the Naval Air Training Command, the Naval Technical Training Command, and the rear admiral in command of the Great Lakes training complex. I learned from them of their frustration with the micro-management from the CNET staff. This was especially true of the technical training command, headed by Rear Admiral Bob Austin, a superb officer, who described instances of his instructors making suggestions for improvements which were denied by the applicable CNET staffer.

After hearing the complaints of the subordinate commanders, I decided that it was necessary to reduce the size of the headquarters staff, and to do so, I needed the support and willing cooperation of the department heads, whom I called into my office individually. Without exception, they each unhesitatingly expressed support and several immediately identified staff billets that should be eliminated in their departments.

Over the course of the next six months or so, through transfers, early retirements, and normal retirements, we eliminated some 200 billets. By not filling billets made vacant by the voluntary departure of the individuals filling those billets, we eventually reduced the staff to about 100 billets. I made it clear to the department heads that their function with regard to the subordinate commanders was to monitor the subordinate commands without interfering, to ensure that CNET objectives were being attained, including high standards in the classroom. They were also the normal points of contact for the commands for which they were responsible. The result was a decentralized organization, with improved morale and production.

CNET was the senior naval officer on the Gulf coast. Consequently, I was often called upon to fill the responsibilities of the Senior Officer Present, a traditional role in the Navy, dating from the days when there were no world-wide means of communications with the mother country, thus those at sea acted on their own in carrying out the mission assigned. However, when in visual range of another Navy vessel, the senior officer present was in charge. In the CNET case, SOP duties included speeches when requested, attending various national holiday celebrations as the Navy representative, and overseeing the security of naval activities in the Gulf states and the states adjacent to them, in the event of a hurricane or any other type of weather that could cause injuries and damage to people and material resources.

Being the wife of the Gulf coast senior naval officer caused similar responsibilities to be placed on Peggy's shoulders. She was very conscientious, and was often in attendance at meetings of women's organizations where her advice was sought on a variety of subjects.

At a meeting of the women's auxiliary of a local veteran's organization, the topic was whether they should march in the upcoming Memorial Day parade, and what kind of uniform dress should they wear? As if on cue, they all turned to Peggy, and the defacto leader of the debate asked Peggy for her opinion. Peggy did not want to take sides, so she thought for a minute, and then told them that the only experience she had with parades was as an onlooker, so she really had no advice to offer, and she added that she was sure that whatever decision was made, such an attractive group of women would be well received in the parade. When she told me about the meeting, she fretted that perhaps she should have offered some advice. I asked her what finally was decided, and she said that they seemed to calm down after her comment, and they voted to take up the questions with their husbands. I told her that she had given them the assurance they needed and had saved them from becoming a group filled with dissension. Seemed to me that she had done pretty well. But week after week of dealing with diverse groups and traveling extensively in response to invitations, was taking its toll of Peggy's endurance. By the time we were entering our third year in Pensacola, Peggy was becoming exhausted.

In the early spring of 1985, on a weekday afternoon, I received a call from the doctor who commanded the naval hospital. She informed me that Peggy was in the hospital for observation, after being driven there by Chief Petty Officer Pura, the steward in charge of our quarters. Peggy had a severe headache that was more than she could bear, so they had sedated her and she was now resting quietly.

I went immediately to the hospital, and was told that after Peggy awoke, they intended to do a series of tests to try to determine what the cause of such a severe pain could be. The doctor said she thought Peggy would sleep for several hours, and suggested I get some dinner and then come back.

When I returned, Peggy was just beginning to awaken, and said she felt much better, indicating that she wanted to go home, but the doctor advised her of the need to do some tests first, to which Peggy reluctantly agreed. The doctor also told her that she would feel better if they could keep her overnight, just to ensure that she was all right. Peggy looked at me, and I nodded in agreement with the doctor.

The next morning, I picked her up and took her home, where she wanted to start getting into her round of activities again. I told her if she did not stay home and get additional rest, I would have to stay there to see that she did. I then called my office and had them cancel all of Peggy's appointments for the rest of the week and the following week as well.

That afternoon, the doctor called me and said that, based on the test results, she had concluded that Peggy was overly tired and needed to rest and cut back on her activities. She also said that Peggy's eyes were in the early stages of glaucoma, and that she needed to see an ophthalmologist without delay in order to get the pressure in her eyes down to a safe level.

Considering all that had happened in the last 24 hours, and given the doctor's diagnosis of exhaustion, I concluded that it was time for me to retire. Previously, the Navy had nominated me for the position of director of the National Security Agency, which rotated among the services. I had been interviewed by the Secretary of Defense, Mr. Weinberger, who gave me an upcheck, and by the Director of National Intelligence, William Casey. The latter had the final word on the appointment, and at the conclusion of our meeting, he said he would approve my appointment. However, the following day, after I had returned to Pensacola, I was informed by the CNO that Casey had disapproved my appointment. In the event, the post went to the Army. I don't know why he changed his mind, but I suspect he called Anne Armstrong, knowing that I had been with the PFIAB, and Anne had probably told him of her disappointment with my apparent attitude.

After my being turned down for NSA, Secretary Lehman informed me that he wanted me to stay in the CNET post for another year, at which time the current admiral at NATO would be retiring, and he intended to name me for the job. I was pleased because it meant a fourth star, and it would be a most interesting place to be. I had not told Peggy, because much can happen to change an assignment in a year, and I did not want her to be disappointed if the proposed move did not eventuate. I may have also been influenced by sensing that she would not be happy to hear that she was faced with another year to be Mrs. Navy to the Gulf Coast. In any case, I now resolved to tell Mr. Lehman of Peggy's condition and inform him of my decision to retire near the end of 1985.

After speaking with Mr. Lehman, who offered his sympathy upon hearing of Peggy's condition, I called CNO and told him I was sending a letter to request retirement on 1 November 1985, and told him why. He also was very understanding, and offered any assistance if needed.

Several weeks later, while on a routine visit to Washington, I was asked to visit the Secretary of Energy. He had been an Assistant Secretary of the Navy while I was Director of the Office of Program Appraisal on the SecNav staff. He told me that he had heard that I was retiring, and offered me the position of Assistant Secretary of Energy for Nuclear Matters, or some such title, which would have placed me in the ironic position of being the superior of the Director of Naval Reactors, Admiral Rickover's post, now filled by Admiral Kin McKee, who had succeeded Rickover when the latter was forced to retire by President Reagan. I was sorely tempted to accept right then but something held me from doing so, and I asked him if I could call him the next day with my decision, to which he agreed. That evening, after I returned to Pensacola, I found Peggy in very good spirits, and she chatted happily about her plans to open an antiques shop in Virginia after I retired. The next morning, I advised the Secretary's executive assistant that I regretfully could not accept his offer

I subsequently was contacted by the head of ACDA, the Arms Control and Disarmament Agency, offering me the position of Deputy Director, and again, I had to decline.

On 1 November 1985, I donned my dress blue uniform for the last time on active duty. In a ceremony held in the Naval Aviation Museum at Pensacola, I retired from the Navy in which I had enlisted on 15 July 1946, thus completing 39 years, 3 months and 18 days in Navy blue.

On that first night in the Navy, when I lay in my bunk, wondering what I had done, little did I realize what lay ahead. My years in the Navy were not without their mistakes and doubts, yet I would do it again in a heart-beat. Now, however, I was re-entering a world I had left so long ago.

Epilogue

Peggy set up her antiques shop in an eighteenth century frame house we bought in Aldie, Virginia. She spent three happy years buying and selling her beloved antiques, but in the spring of 1989, she began to have difficulty with writing and maintaining her shop records. The doctors at Georgetown University Hospital concluded, after a series of tests given her, that she was in the early stages of Alzheimer's Disease.

The devastating effects of Alzheimer's inexorably reduced Peggy's ability to do normal activities, to the point that I could no longer care for her properly. We had sold "Maidstone" and had bought a condominium in Timonium, Maryland, where Peggy could be near her sisters. That was in August of 1993, but by March of 1994, it was necessary for Peggy to enter Brightwood, a nursing facility in the area. Leaving my dear Peggy there was the hardest thing I ever had to do. On 22 February, 2002, Peggy succumbed to the effects of Alzheimer's, after a valiant struggle lasting thirteen years.

In December of 1987, we had lost our son, Mark, in an aircraft accident in the Mojave Desert of California while serving in the Marine Corps, and now Peggy was gone also. Tragedy, suffering and death, are all part of life, and must be accepted as such. People ask why our Creator allows suffering and death, and although Judeo-Christian theology offers answers, most of us still do not really understand. For my part, I see the process of aging, with its attendant aches and ills, as God's way to break us away from the attractions of this life in order for us to prepare for the eternity that awaits us. But what of the death of a young person like Mark? Why does that happen? I believe that God asks us to have faith in His mercy and His wisdom, so some things cannot be explained in a human way, but must be accepted as part of God's plans for us.

I hope my grandchildren will take time to see how blessed we, as a family, have been. I married the girl who stole my heart while we were still in high school. Our children have been a joy, and my three daughters are the gems in my life. I have the pleasure of watching twelve grandchildren evolve into adults who hopefully will reflect the values instilled in them by their parents. And as a great-grandfather of five* more offspring in the family, I see God's promise that life will go on.

James A. Sagerholm
Vice Admiral, USN (Ret.)
31 January 2015

*Now six, with a seventh due in January 2016.

CPSIA information can be obtained
at www.ICGtesting.com
Printed in the USA
FFOW02n1345201015
17844FF